PRAISE FOR CHRIS LEE
AND *TRANSFORM YOUR LIFE*

Meeting Chris Lee was a turning point for me. He gave me the gift of tools to build a better version of myself, and for that, I will be forever grateful. Sharing his knowledge through this book is what represents Chris' heart. And we receive it with open arms—more tools, more to build a better life for ourselves and our loved ones. By giving of ourselves, we create abundance, abundance of love, our most important commodity and treasure. We're ready! Bring it on, Chris!

Ednita Nazario
Grammy-nominated International
Singer and Broadway Actress

Chris Lee is one of the best trainers, personal coaches, and human beings on the planet. He has spent the last three decades passionately committed and dedicated to inspiring thousands of people throughout the world to discover their dreams. His book, *Transform your Life*, is a must read! It is a true honor and privilege to have Chris on your team.

Michael Strasner
Transformational Coach and Trainer and #1 Bestselling
Author of *Living on the Skinny Branches*

Transform your Life, Chris Lee's most recent book is a gift of his wisdom that he has transmitted to thousands of people all around the world. The 10 principles in this book have served me when the economic crisis knocked on my door. I went from a bankruptcy to creating success, T.V shows, radio shows, 10 bestsellers, and a wonderful relationship with my children and my wife. This book is a critical tool to live an abundant and prosperous life. Thank you Chris.

Silverio Perez
Author, Producer, Musician, Motivator & Host of
Univision Puerto Rico: Que es Lo Que Hay?

D0067264

Chris Lee is a transformational guru. His honest concern, compassion, and kindness to others make him such an inspirational leader. *Transform Your Life: 10 Principles of Abundance and Prosperity* is full of inspiration, valuable insights, and useful information that will lead you on the road to success. Everyone will benefit from this book. His writing is powerful and practical. I feel honored to share the microphone with him in my national radio show every week.

Maria Marin
Bestselling Author, TV & Radio Personality

In our 17 years of partnership, mentoring and co-creation in our shared vision of coaching and training EQ Transformation, Chris is an irreplaceable, one-of-a-kind, wholehearted genius friend driven by his passion to transform lives.

After learning these 10 simple principles of how to create love, friendship, relationships, money and time, they are all limitless and accessible to me...

Simple, abundance is a mindfulness I live in.

This is a must-read for all seekers of unlimited access to Abundance & Prosperity, which all begins with GRATITUDE for what we have.

Robyn Williams
Founder and C.E.O Choicecenter Leadership
University Las Vegas, Nevada

Chris provided an opportunity for me to see myself as others do and have a deeper understanding of what works and what doesn't work. It has helped me to be the best version of myself on a more consistent basis. From a career standpoint, the tools I learned were priceless. I broke through self-limiting beliefs that I couldn't compete with the younger players in the world. Once I did, within months, I once again became the #1 ranked poker player in the world. Chris made it clear to me that if it was to be, it was going to be up to me."

Daniel Negraneu
#1 Ranked Poker Player in the World and
Poker Hall of Fame Inductee

I met Chris during a very hard break up, and he immediately felt like family to me. Chris is excellent at listening, but even more than that, he was a guiding light during a dark long journey. He is my coach, but he's also one of my best friends. He adds so much to my life. He helps me with business decisions as passionately as he helps me in my personal life. I recommend *Transform Your Life: 10 Principles of Abundance and Prosperity* because his wisdom has enriched my life and I'd love others to experience the same. There's never a cap on personal growth, and this book is a treasure.

Nadine Velazquez
Actress and Producer

Chris Lee is not only one of my best friends, he gave me the tools to get my joy and smile back.

Pauley Shore
Comedian, Actor, Producer,
Director and owner of *The Comedy Store*

I have known Chris Lee for over 20 years not only as a trainer but also as one of my closest friends. I have seen his own personal growth and witnessed how he has touched so many people around the world with is gift. Chris has touched me and has always been there in every critical moment of my life and career with the right words, coaching and support to move forward with my dreams.

This book will be a gift to everyone who reads it because it's a practical easy to apply guide to achieve your dreams. This book teaches you that there are no obstacles bigger than your vision! Not only will you become more successful in your goals you will also become a successful human being.

Julian Gil
Actor, Producer and Presenter

Chris Lee is an extremely experienced and gifted trainer with an uncanny ability to create extraordinary results with his clients, including myself. He has been my personal mentor and his coaching has lead to abundance in my relationships and in my business. Mostly importantly, all the growth came along with less stress and greater happiness. Priceless! I am grateful to have had the fortune of learning from this master of transformation. I have witnessed his work with hundreds of students and he always delivers. Every time he speaks, breakthroughs follow and people take their lives to the next level. This book is a powerful tool for anyone ready to take their destiny into their own hands and create the life of their dreams.

Chris Hawker
Owner, Trident Design and Next Level

Chris Lee is one of my closest friends and has always been there for me. I highly recommend his book, *Transform Your Life 10*: Principles of Abundance and Prosperity because it is a simple, yet powerful, easy to read guide to an abundant life! The principles established in this book are proven to work to create the life we are meant to have! This book is filled with practical wisdom. Enjoy the book and have a blessed life.

Barbara Bermudo
Anchor, Primer Impacto Univision

Chris Lee has been a mentor, friend and confidante for over 20 years. When nobody else saw the trainer in me, Chris did. Chris is a man guided by love and commitment. He is outrageous, a risk taker and stood for me to create what I thought was an impossible future. This is what is going to happen for you, if you allow yourself. If you are ready to create an abundant, joyful, and extraordinary life, this book is for you.

Ivette Rodriguez,
Trainer and Author of the bestselling book,
Cuentos De Tu Loca Mensajes De Tu Sabia

Chris is a true friend – something rare in this day and age. No matter how much time we are apart, we share the same trust, love, and support. Chris's support has been unconditional, and his emotional wisdom, has supported me during difficult times. *Transform Your Life* will have a major impact in your life, because it affirms that the power is within us. When we apply the 10 principles of abundance and prosperity with commitment and strength, we can accomplish everything that we dream of.

Luz Garcia
Entrepreneur, Producer and Creator of the TV Show,
"Noches De Luz"

In life you meet people who can change your life around. If I had to describe my friend Chris Lee in one word, it would be *passion*. It is this passion that has taken him all over the world the past 20 years offering transformational workshops. This book is a guide for everyone who is committed to achieving his or her vision and dreams. One of my favorite points of this book is the attitude of gratitude. Gratitude is the key to abundance and prosperity. With this awareness, we learn that the impossible is possible.

- Barbara Serrano, Financial Advisor and Author of *Rica...*
Libertad Financiera Para La Mujer

Chris Lee once again has created something phenomenal. This book describes step by step how you can implement abundance in every aspect of your life. The moment you open this book you can't stop reading till the last page is down. It's a must read for everyone. It will create a profound shift of your consciousness of your prosperity and abundance in love and money.

Margo Majdi
CEO of Mastery in Transformational Training
and Author of *The Art of Acknowledgement*

To download a free gift of *Abundance and Prosperity* in PDF format, go to www.ChrisLeeMotivator.com.
Don't delay—visit www.ChrisLeeMotivator.com and get your free gift right now!

Transform Your

LIFE

10 PRINCIPLES OF ABUNDANCE AND PROSPERITY

CHRIS LEE

Transform Your Life
Ten Principles of Abundance and Prosperity
Chris Lee

Copyright © 2016

Printed in the United States of America
ISBN-13:978-0-692-67630-1

This book is dedicated to my mother, the one person who has always seen the masterpiece in me since the day I was born.

I also dedicate this book to the thousands of students I have had the honor to serve through my transformational workshops since 1988.

FOREWORD

IN THE SUMMER of 2013, I enrolled in a transformational leadership workshop in Los Angeles at the recommendation of my good friend, Quddus. Chris Lee, a transformation coach I had never heard of, was the facilitator. The workshop focuses on developing emotional intelligence—one of the most important ingredients for achieving next level success. This is true with high-performing athletes, championship coaches, business executives, and anyone, really.

Of course, I had no idea then that those few days would forever alter the trajectory of my life.

I was already at the top of my game in my career, but there was an ever-present nagging feeling in the back of my mind that nothing I did was ever good enough. I was accomplishing everything I wanted to, but with each triumph, I felt deflated again and again. Something was missing, and I didn't know what it was or that I could ever find it.

The information Chris Lee taught me became the framework for a more empowering paradigm in my life. What was once out of reach now seemed possible. My family relationships were strengthened, new opportunities opened up, my business grew, and my emotional world expanded. I no longer viewed myself

XII • CHRIS LEE

as a victim of my past and instead decided to take on my life in a whole new way.

It's amazing what flows our way when we shift the way we think and our physical way of being. I learned that if we aren't receiving all of the things we want, then most likely there are a number of things holding us back. There's a way to change this dilemma, and it starts with your *mindset*. Chris showed me that I am 100% responsible for my life and every aspect of it and that I am the author of my own story.

It didn't take long for me to realize that Lee was a master of his craft. Here was a man you could hardly find if you Googled him, and yet his ability to move and inspire people was mind-blowing. On par with the best thought leaders I have ever heard speak, Chris gifted me with tools that have been unlocking my most extraordinary life ever since.

Chris Lee's transformation coaching has profoundly impacted the lives of hundreds of thousands of people over the past three decades. He is a tireless, generous force for positive change in the world and a relentless champion for world peace. For all of his success as a businessman and coach, he could have retired ten years ago and lived happily ever after on the beach. Instead, he travels the world seemingly non-stop like a "maniac on a mission," literally saving people's lives and waking people up to their unique gifts. Chris has been the catalyst for countless service projects, charity campaigns, and other radical acts of kindness all over the world.

A while ago, I wondered how it could be that Chris didn't have a significant online presence or even a website of which to speak. I thought he should certainly be more widely recognized, because he is every bit as brilliant and impactful as the most well-known names in personal development, if not more so. When I asked him why that was, he replied that he never saw a need for it. I marveled at the fact that Chris does what he does without any pursuit of fame or recognition—which he could certainly obtain at any moment. He does his work like a silent magician, outside the radar of the public eye, and never leaves a place the way he found it, but better.

A short two years after that life-changing workshop, Chris has become a dear friend, mentor, and is now my personal coach. I am constantly learning and growing under his tutelage. I can say with confidence that the successes I have had since meeting him have been some of the most significant achievements of my life. Chris Lee's coaching is *that powerful.* The outrageous goals I set for myself, like interviewing one of my idols, Anthony Robbins, on my podcast, *The School of Greatness,* securing a substantial advance for a book deal with a major publisher, selling a company for seven figures, and even entering into a loving and healthy romantic relationship, are all due to the direct influence of this great man.

Ten Principles of Abundance and Prosperity featuring Chris Lee is one of most popular podcast episodes on *The School of Greatness.* In it, Chris spoke about the principles that he expands on in this book. He continues to be my most popular guest and has been featured eight times (and counting), bringing incredible content

XIV • CHRIS LEE

every time. His interviews have been downloaded over 350,000 times.

As Chris says, abundance isn't about what you have, but *who you are*. He teaches that abundance is a state of consciousness—the consciousness of gratitude—and prosperity is a result of that consciousness. Chris Lee is a man who embodies these principles.

I guarantee, if you allow it and put these principles into practice, the contents of this book will change your life. They have and continue to influence mine each and every day. Chris Lee is a one of a kind, amazing man, whom I would trust with my life. I encourage you to open your hearts and minds to his wisdom and experience so that you, too, can live your best life—a life of beautiful, unlimited abundance and prosperity.

Lewis Howes
New York Times Bestselling Author
of *The School of Greatness*

"Our **deepest fear** is not that we are inadequate. Our **deepest fear** is that we are powerful beyond measure. It is our light, not our darkness, that most frightens us. We ask ourselves, who am I to be brilliant, gorgeous, talented and fabulous? Actually who are we not to be? You are a child of God. Your playing small doesn't serve the world. There is nothing enlightened about shrinking so that other people won't feel insecure around you. We are all meant to shine as children do. We were born to make manifest the glory of God that is within us. It's not just in some of us; it's in everyone. And when we let our own light shine, we unconsciously give other people permission to do the same. As we are liberated from our own fear, our presence automatically liberates others."

- Marianne Williamson

TABLE OF CONTENTS

INTRODUCTION

"I cursed the fact I had no shoes until I saw a man with no feet …"

– Ancient Persian Proverb

SOCIETY HATES LACK. We always want more—more fame, more money, more clout, more love, more color, more beauty, and time in our lives. Yet, it seems that the more we try to acquire those things, the farther and farther away they seem to move away from us. Naturally, after spending so much time and energy trying to catch what seems so far beyond our reach, we resign ourselves to a mediocre life, an average life, a life of struggle and stress. We settle for so much less than the extraordinary success, fulfillment, and unbridled joy that we are meant to experience.

Life is meant to be lived with joy and passion. It's an experience beyond the wildest imagination when we seize and embrace all the abundance that it has to offer. We're supposed to share our passions and gifts freely and with abandon so that others can benefit from the uniqueness that lies within each of us. Life is about connecting, with each other and the universe, in a way that we know we belong—we are a part of this thing called the bigger picture. Not only are we part of it, but our contributions add a stroke of beauty to it. As we create the masterpiece that is within us, we bring new color and life to those around us.

Even though abundance and prosperity can be attained by every one of us, far too few of us manage to attract it into our lives. One of the things I keep hearing in my workshops is how people don't have enough money, time, love, or energy to do or have what they want. There is a scarcity conversation all across the board and all over the world as people accept that their status quo is sealed for eternity. Our lives don't have to be that way. Every single person in this glorious universe has the opportunity to create abundance and prosperity in their life. Anything less isn't due to circumstance, destiny, or the unfair hand that we believe has been dealt. It's because people are going about it the wrong way. They don't think they're worthy of more, they're not clear about what they want, and they don't want it badly enough.

What people don't realize is that it's a lot easier than they think to create an abundant and prosperous life. It's shifting a mindset. Everything, without a single exception, is mindset, and when you shift your mindset from scarcity and lack to abundance and prosperity, your reality shifts. When your reality shifts, your actions and choices shift; therefore, your results shift.

Some may believe they already know this, but knowing it is not the same as living it—*really* living it and practicing it every day. Some of you have heard some of the life-changing principles I'm about to share, but you don't implement them faithfully and rigorously throughout your lives. Some of you are already embodying these principles and are benefiting from them, but you think it was just luck. Some of you have to start from the beginning, finding and learning what is holding you back and discovering how to shift the results you're receiving to the ones you really want.

This book is about awakening the already-existing abundance that is within you. By waking up that abundance that you were born with—yes, you were born with abundance, it's already in you—and becoming loyal to it, the result is prosperity. If you live by the specific principles of abundance and prosperity in an organic way, you'll be blown away by the results they produce. They will change your life forever. Believe me, great things are about to happen, but you have to be willing to let them happen.

Scarcity was instilled into me at a young age. The youngest of five children, I was born in Long Island, New York. When I was two years old, my parents moved our family to Puerto Rico to pursue business opportunities. When I was six, my dad abandoned us. I later found out that he went to prison in New York for embezzlement.

My mom was left to raise and support five children on her own. Imagine for a moment a single mother raising five children in a foreign country and not knowing the language. There was no money. However, my mom never gave up. She managed to make sure there was always food on the table and we got a good education. At the time, we lived in a three-bedroom apartment— Mom slept on the couch, and the five of us shared the bedrooms.

Yet, there was never enough; there was never enough money or enough time. The one thing that was plentiful was fear and scarcity. Mom worked various jobs to earn money to support us. She taught bridge lessons, worked in sales and advertising, and found other odd jobs to provide for our family. Still, our lives centered around lack. I grew up feeling like I wasn't enough and would never have enough. The scarcity mindset in our house was very real.

Our circumstances changed when I turned ten. My mom married the man who became my stepfather, and we moved in with him. The content of our lives changed, but not the context. I still felt like a poor, little abandoned boy. I missed my father, blamed my mother, and hated my stepfather. I always felt like I was "less than" everyone else. Burdened with these limiting beliefs, my teenage years were a nightmare, for me and everyone near me. I was kicked out of schools and was always in trouble. Fortunately, with the support of my mother and stepfather and their unwavering belief in me, I managed to graduate from high school and was accepted into Northeastern University in Boston.

Though I was now in college, I still struggled with limiting beliefs, like "I'm not good enough," "I don't matter," "I will never have enough … love, time, money, worth." It's these conversations and interpretations that kept me in scarcity. At this time, I was working at the Chart House in Boston and making a lot of money, about $200 a night, which was a lot of money back then. For the first time, I saw that I could really make money, even more than most waiters because of my generous nature. I was authentically joyful, loving, and caring with all of my customers. Due to this rapport I'd built with them, they would come back to the restaurant and always request to sit in my assigned section.

But money wasn't enough to chase away scarcity. I still had old beliefs that kept scarcity alive—underlying beliefs that I'd end up on the street, be abandoned again, or struggle like my mom had for so many years. I was making money, but I never saved any of it. Instead, I spent it all, falling into a hoard-then-spend cycle and habit. I didn't think I deserved money or abundance. I hadn't yet had my breakthrough.

It wasn't until I was invited by a friend to participate in a transformational workshop that I began to learn the tools of abundance and prosperity. Admittedly, I went to the event just because my friends were going. I didn't expect much from it and certainly didn't anticipate that it would change my life. I was a skeptic—at that time, I held the world title. However, it ended up being the best thing I ever did and one of the most valuable tools I've ever received—so much so that, today, I lead these workshops across the world.

What turned me around and made me a believer? During one of the workshops, I was asked to journal my vision and the specific results I was committed to creating for my future, which was a stretch for me because I wasn't much of a writer. For me, sitting down and focusing to write—with an actual pen and paper— was a chore. In that journal, I had to pen my future and create a ten-year game plan. So I wrote down my goals, all along laughing at the absurdity of them—like, yeah, that's really gonna happen! Right.

A month later, I lost the journal. At that time in my life, I was a gypsy, living from place to place. I kept moving, and moving, and moving. Eventually, I gave up on finding it and forgot about it. Twelve years later, I found the journal in a box, within a box, within a box. I opened it up, thinking it would be very interesting to see what I had written.

I was floored to see that every single declaration I had made in the workshop had become reality 12 years later. Every single one. Wow! I didn't skip one. I said I'd be a trainer, did that. I said I'd bring my family together, did that. I said I'd be financially free, did that. I said I'd meet the love of my life—did that (many times). Oh, yes, I can't deny the abundance!

Like I said, I was a skeptic when I was writing those declarations, but I went along with the exercise and played the game. Sometimes our own beliefs stop us from dreaming or declaring big. I think that's because we're all afraid to make it and achieve it—whatever "it" is. We spend far too much of our lives apologizing for our gifts and talents. In this book, you'll learn how to overcome that, as well.

Today, I fully embrace the principles of abundance and prosperity. They work. I am the living, breathing, abundant, and prosperous proof! I'd always wanted the life I'm living but never in my wildest dreams thought it was possible. What I didn't know was I was just ten principles away from attracting it into my life. I had spent years chasing a future that had become increasingly more elusive, when all I had to do was attract it into my life. It was already there. It was always there. But until I learned these life-changing principles, it was hidden from me.

You, too, have the power, the capability, and the potential to create a life of overwhelming abundance and prosperity. This book is a powerful, life-defining opportunity. You have the power to create the life you want. Like I always say, "If you have the capacity to dream it, you can create it." You are about to embark on ten monumental principles that will transform your life. When you implement them, you'll find that you no longer have to pursue what you want in life—what you want will pursue you. Let the journey begin!

TWEET THIS:
"Abundance is a state of consciousness,
Prosperity is the result of that consciousness"
#TransformYourLife @ChrisMotivador

Chapter One

WHAT IS ABUNDANCE AND PROSPERITY?

TWEET THIS:
"Self Worth = Net Worth."
– #TransformYourLife @ChrisMotivador

PEOPLE OFTEN MISUNDERSTAND abundance and prosperity. They typically assume that it equates to how much we have—in the form of money and material possessions. How much money do we make, what types of cars do we drive, and how high have we climbed up the corporate ladder? That is the first problem that we must address—we need to correct our mistaken definitions of abundance and prosperity and define what they really are.

You are abundant. *Already.* At this very minute. It's true. In fact, you're a billionaire—you just don't know it. There are so many things in your life that are priceless that you wouldn't trade for anything in the world. If I were to give you a million dollars and take away one of your most treasured qualities, would you sell it? Would you give up your eyesight or your hearing for financial independence? Would you trade your most treasured asset or trait for power or fame? Most people wouldn't.

We don't want to get rid of something that is valued and important to us. And we shouldn't have to.

We're already abundant because we have something that is priceless in our lives. Like the saying goes, we complain that we don't have shoes until we meet a man with no feet. We are fortunate in so many wonderful ways. Yet, we still focus on the things we don't have, rather than the things we do have.

Abundance is knowing, really knowing, that we already have everything we need, and that we are already enough. But we cannot tap into it because we're going about it the wrong way. The universe isn't responding because we misunderstand what abundance is and how to attract it into our lives.

First, abundance, true abundance, is about being grateful for being here and acknowledging and appreciating everything good in our lives.

Let's really look at abundance and get clear on what it means.

What is Abundance?

Most people think abundance is having a lot of money, time, cars, and material things. That's not abundance. That's nothing more than a lot of stuff. Abundance isn't stuff—you have to have abundance *before* you can get that stuff. That stuff that sits in our driveways, graces our homes, and adorns our bodies are just things—and they are a byproduct of abundance, not the definition of it.

You can take away any of those things and still be abundant. There are so many things I have that I wouldn't trade for any amount of money, and at the end of the day, neither would you. You are already abundant! You are breathing. You can read. You can talk. You can see. You can feel. You have things that money cannot buy— you are, indeed, already abundant.

Abundance is about being grateful for what you have—not just a halfhearted appreciation, but really owning it. If you really, truly felt that and lived it, there would be no room for complaining, anger, and sorrow in your life. You could lose $100,000, but still know that you're abundant—you didn't lose your legs or your eyesight. Hallelujah! Yes! I only lost $100,000! You see, true abundance has everything to do with how you see the world, and it has to do with who you are. It's about shifting consciousness. And that is the best definition of abundance I can give you: it is a state of consciousness.

When you live from a place of gratitude and appreciation, you can shift your consciousness quickly from a place of scarcity to a place of abundance. It sounds too simple, but I'm here to tell you that I know it works. You cannot have what you want until you are grateful for what you have. Stop for just a minute and read that sentence one more time. You cannot have what you want until you are grateful for what you have.

This is one of the most profound things you will ever learn. And until you embrace it and implement this life-changing practice in your life, you will not be privileged to experience true abundance and prosperity. It simply won't happen.

The state of abundance is gratefulness. What do you have to be grateful for? How about the fact that you're breathing? Think about all the people who can't breathe without a tube or a mask. You can focus on the fact that you can see, listen, walk, and talk. All of you who are reading this can focus on the fact that you are blessed with something to read, the time to read it, and the ability to do so.

Say thank you. Wow, I'm blessed. It's a new day! I do have something to be grateful for, after all.

Abundance is living life on a different platform. Abundance is a state of being. It's a state of consciousness centered around a pillar of gratitude and generosity. When you are generous and grateful, life will be generous and grateful with you. Always. When you come from gratitude and gratefulness and acknowledge all of the immense gifts that you have as a human being, your life will change forever.

What is Prosperity?

Prosperity is the multiplication of the blessings and abundance in our lives. It is not the same as abundance. Abundance is the mindset, and prosperity is the *result* of the consciousness of abundance. In my opinion, prosperity represents the things we are meant to have, but we don't have them because we go about getting them in the wrong way.

Most people come from scarcity. The old example is seeing the glass half-empty versus seeing the glass half-full. We see through our lenses the things we don't have, what we don't create, and what we need but can't seem to acquire, and because our mind is like a magnet, it gravitates to produce precisely what we see.

Unfortunately, most of us embrace scarcity, which is the opposite of what we want to do. In fact, we not only hang onto it, we defend it, giving excuses for why we can't give it up. Of course, we don't see it that way, but there's no question about it—scarcity is a belief that has been ingrained in us and accepted by us. Not only do we accept it, we are guilty of not allowing it to disappear.

The following scenario is one I hear often and one that might resonate with you.

Chris, I can't seem to get ahead. I've tried and tried, but nothing is working. I grew up with parents who were on a never-ending struggle to make ends meet. Dad was a blue-collar worker who lived less than paycheck to paycheck. There was never enough money, and we were always reminded that we couldn't afford this or couldn't do that. When I grew up, I vowed I wasn't going to live like that. I wanted my family to have a better life, a life that wasn't so hard. But no matter what I do, the cycle seems to be repeating itself. What am I doing wrong?

My response:

I'm not going to sugar coat this, because you need to hear it and take it to heart. You are your father. You have become your father. You grew up with and adopted the "not enough" mentality. You can't make enough money, you don't have enough things, and you're always falling short of what you want. You have adopted the scarcity mentality and are repeating your father's struggles all over again. If you want to stop this cycle and invite abundance and prosperity into your life, you MUST, absolutely MUST, stop chasing it and start being grateful for what you have. Stop making excuses for why things are the way they are … and then want abundance and prosperity enough that you're committed to attracting them into your life.

What you think about expands. If you think about what you don't have—"I don't have money"—or if you think about what you haven't created—"I haven't gotten that job yet" or "I haven't created that relationship yet"—your mind gravitates toward that and it snowballs, so the only reality you'll know is what you don't have. Nothing changes … or you get more of what you don't really want!

We chase prosperity, we chase clients and sales, we chase relationships and careers. We chase money. But the more we chase those things, the faster they run away from us. What would happen if we reverse that cycle and instead of chasing things, start attracting them? Imagine the things we want just coming to us for no reason other than we feel we deserve them. Wow. Now, that's powerful.

What are you attracting? What is your self-worth? The two go hand in hand. Your net worth equals your self-worth. If you don't feel you deserve what you want or don't think you're good enough, smart enough, rich enough, or educated enough, you'll attract those results. Groucho Marx once said, "I would never be a member of any club that would have me as a member." Would you date you? Would you invest money in you? Your self-worth will determine that.

You must start first with abundance, which is a way of being—a way of living. Prosperity is the byproduct. You cannot have prosperity without abundance. It cannot and will not happen.

It's impossible to create prosperity from a broken foundation. No matter what we put in that broken foundation, it's cracked and it's never enough. I know millionaires who live in scarcity. For example, I have a friend who makes over a million dollars a month, and he's the most negative, depressed person. He doesn't trust anybody, isn't joyful, and, sadly, he isn't free. He says things like, "Everyone is using me." "I can't trust people." "The IRS is after me." It's just amazing how he won't get that his joy does not come from his money; it comes from who he's being. My coaching to him is to be grateful for all the things that are priceless in his life. In the end, those are the only things that are going to matter, not the money.

I also know people who don't make a lot of money, but they're totally abundant, because they live in gratitude and appreciation. So it's really not about what you have, it's about who you are.

Practice Abundance

We focus on what we don't have, what we haven't created, and what we haven't accomplished. That's the scarcity mentality of "not enough." It's a negative energy that pushes away all the things we're seeking. Instead of attracting it or gravitating toward it, we're doing the exact opposite and pushing it away.

The state of abundance is that consciousness of waking up every day, opening your eyes, and saying, "Thank you." Thank you, God. Thank you, universe. Thank you for today. Thank you for everything I have.

I'm grateful. That's the first exercise in this book. Every single day when you wake up, open your eyes and just say the words "thank you," because that will start your day in an abundant way. You're saying, "Thank you. I arrived at another day."

I do that when I wake up every day. I'm like, "Wow, I made it! I'm still here!" I don't take life for granted, because every day, there are people who don't get to wake up. Just like when I'm flying and the airplane lands, I rejoice, "Yes, I made it! Thank you." It's not just something I talk about. I live this. I truly live it and practice it religiously.

The next time you're having a moment and realize you're not happy, thinking that life is throwing you a curve ball or that things aren't turning out the way you'd like, remember that you still have something to be grateful for. For example, when you're stuck in traffic and upset, ready to punch your fist through the windshield, or would love to release your frustrations in a moment of vengeful road rage against another driver, remember there will be a day when you can't drive. There will be a day when you wish you had somewhere to go. There will be a day when you can't go anywhere.

Like when my stepfather was on his death bed, he said, "You know what? Everything I complained about is actually a luxury. I wish I had those things to complain about again. Actually, when I was in traffic, it meant I was going somewhere, and now I'm stuck in this bed."

What's good or bad in our lives is nothing more than an interpretation. We choose the interpretation. We are always at choice—we can choose a negative interpretation or a positive one. It's up to us. Be grateful, emphatically grateful, for everything in life and really see it as a blessing. When you see life as a blessing, the door to abundance and prosperity will open for you. It's always been there, but your state of consciousness has not allowed you to see it.

The good, the bad, the ugly in life are all blessings. Even life's breakdowns are lessons in disguise. Believe it or not, even the harshest conditions can be blessings in disguise, but it's up to you to see it from that perspective. When you do, you'll open the door to abundance and prosperity. For example, Viktor Frankle, the author of *A Man's Search for Meaning*, found his freedom in a concentration camp. In conclusion, remember, abundance is not about money or things. Abundance is a state of mind. It's having enough and being grateful and feeling blessed for what you do have.

When you achieve that state and live it every day, you'll find prosperity. Prosperity is the byproduct or result of abundance. When you focus on what you've been given and all that is good, you'll get more of it. That's how the universe works. It's been that way since the dawn of time. But if you focus on what you don't have, the universe will bring more of the same. It's non-discriminatory.

The principles you're about to learn are game changers. They will take you to places you've never imagined. They will help you attract love, financial freedom, peace, contentment, health, and prestige — whatever it is that you want. But only if you're committed to it and want it bad enough.

Are you ready? Let's go.

PRACTICE GRATITUDE:

TWEET THIS:
"When I live in gratitude, life will give me more
to be grateful for."
#TransformYourLife @ChrisMotivador

List ten things you are grateful for:

1. _____

2. _____

3. _____

4. _____

5. _____

6. _____

7. _____

8. _____

9. _____

10. _____

Chapter Two

PRINCIPLE 1:
THE PRINCIPLE OF GIVING

> "**The purpose of life is to discover your gift.** The work of life is to develop it. The meaning **of life is to give your gift away.**"
> – David S. Viscott, *Finding Your Strength in Difficult Times: A Book of Meditations*

THE FIRST PRINCIPLE is giving. This is the most fundamental principle upon which all others are based. Giving is the natural tendency of life. When you give freely, what comes back is multiplied. Giving is a way of living. Giving is manifested by sharing, contributing, serving, loving, and caring.

Giving is a river that continually flows. By adopting this principle, you get to be Miss or Mr. Generosity with all of your magical qualities and talents—not just sometimes, but all of the time. Yes, all of the time. Not only when you feel like it—but always. When you are generous with the world, the world will be generous with you. Giving is not optional if you want abundance and prosperity in your life. A giver gives without conditions, not just when they feel like it, or when the circumstances are right, but always. Giving is valuing yourself and your contribution and giving it *freely and willingly.* Think of it as if you have an endless supply and the more you give, the more it is replenished. You are a gift to yourself and to others. You're a rock star. You're lovable, talented, and giving. When you're conscious that you are a gift, that everything in your life is a blessing, and you're conscious that abundance is really a state of gratitude and being grateful, then the natural tendency is to give it away.

Giving is to focus out. Focus on the people around you. Focus on your children. Focus on your partner. Focus on colleagues at work. Wherever you go, be a giver.

There are two kinds of people in life. There are givers and takers. I truly firmly believe in the law of attraction, that what you put out comes back multiplied. For example, in 1979, Mother Teresa won the Nobel Peace Prize for 30 years of giving to the poor and sick in India. She used the entire $190,000 prize to build more homes for the destitute, especially lepers. She called her prize a "gift for the poor." Today, she leaves a legacy of giving that never stops.

The day we die, we take nothing with us. What matters is what we leave behind. When we give out of the pure joy of giving, the actual getting is the giving.

We truly do attract into our lives who we are, what we think, what we speak, and who we're being. So if what you want in life is a joyful, loving, passionate, successful life, then you've got to start giving love, joy, and passion away.

Giving requires that you acknowledge all the things that are working about you. Yes, you have good, amazing qualities and traits. It requires that you acknowledge the things of which you're proud. By acknowledging your own worth, value, and accomplishments, you can authentically share them and build from them.

Practice Giving

There are two ways of thinking in life. One is "What's in it for me?" and the other way of thinking is "What can I contribute?" If you wake up saying, "Thank you. What can I contribute today?" versus "What's today going to do for me?" you've unlocked the consciousness of giving. Give your smile, give a hug, give acknowledgement, go out of your way to make a difference, perform random acts of kindness, brighten someone's day. Share yourself with the world. Sing on the subway so everyone can enjoy your beautiful voice. Give it away—there's enough and more where it came from.

When you do that, you activate the abundance consciousness and the abundance state around you, so things will suddenly start flowing your way. You'll probably have no idea how it happened and will be floored and amazed at the fact that it really is happening. I mean it. Checks will be coming in the mail. People will be offering you jobs. Relationships will start to appear because you're going to show up in a way that creates a container for success in business, love, money, and joy.

When people come from contribution in business— service and giving in business—your business becomes irresistible to other people. So if you want to have an irresistible business and become an irresistible entrepreneur, you've got to be an irresistible person. By being a person who practices giving, you'll start generating abundance everywhere you go and with everyone you meet.

Being generous is about allowing the love and joy in your heart and the gifts that are so uniquely yours to come out into the open so you can share them with others. It stems from self-worth, and you're the only one who can give yourself that self-worth. Self-worth does not come from compliments or praise. It doesn't require awards and validation. Self-worth comes from only one place—you.

Giving is acknowledging all of your amazing abilities. It's telling yourself that you are a pro, a rock star, the queen or king. You matter, to yourself and to others. You are *worthy*.

When you practice giving, you validate your gifts, your talents, and your value in the world. When you share it freely and unconditionally, it comes back to you tenfold. I always say that if you treat others well, they'll treat you well—most of the time. If you treat others like a piece of dirt, hey, they're going to treat you like dirt, too—most of the time. It's like a boomerang—you send beautiful qualities, gifts, and talents out to others, and it comes right back to you. There is no better or more fulfilling way to create abundance.

Sometimes we discount our accomplishments by saying, "That was lucky," or "It was chance." For you to be able to give, you've got to acknowledge what you have to give. For example, what are your talents? What are you good at? Are you an amazing cook? Are you a good dancer? Are you the queen of salsa? Are you good at organizing? Are you a great coach? No matter how mediocre you might feel it is, it's something you can do that others might not be able to do as well. Acknowledge it and give it away. Be the kind of person that is giving.

Create a list of ten of your talents and abilities. Don't confuse these for ways of being, such as I'm loving, I'm happy all of the time. What are you good at? Are you an amazing lover, a great caretaker, a rock star writer? Are you a good parent or a phenomenal speaker? Everyone has thousands (yes, thousands) of things they are amazing at. Give yourself credit and list ten of them.

PRACTICE GIVING

TWEET THIS:
"When I give without expectations, what comes back
is unexpected and multiplied."
#TransformYourLife @ChrisMotivador

List your top 10 talents and skills.

1. _____

2. _____

3. _____

4. _____

5. _____

6. _____

7. _____

8. _____

9. _____

10. _____

PRACTICE GIVING

List your top 10 accomplishments.

1. _____

2. _____

3. _____

4. _____

5. _____

6. _____

7. _____

8. _____

9. _____

10. _____

When you are generous with the world, the world will be generous with you. #TransformYourLife

Find an organization that aligns with your values and principles and volunteer. For example, the Make-a-Wish Foundation (www.wish.org), St. Jude (www.StJude.org), etc.

Chapter Three

PRINCIPLE 2:
LETTING GO

"Life teaches you the art of letting go in every event. When you have learnt to let go, you will be joyful, and as you start being joyful, more will be given to you."

– SRI SRI RAVI SHANKAR

THE SECOND PRINCIPLE of abundance and prosperity is letting go, also known as clearing. Letting go means you're clearing the past. It's not just getting something off your chest in the emotional moment you're in right now. It's a mental, spiritual, and emotional process intended to clear away beliefs and barriers, which limit your ability to create prosperity in your life. You might clear away doubts, feelings, fears, attitudes, and assumptions. Letting go is moving forward by clearing negative energy and forgiving yourself and others.

In this chapter, you will learn how to clear all of the paralyzing and fixed beliefs that you have surrounding money, relationships, and accomplishments. Any negative feeling you are carrying will interfere with abundance and reinforce scarcity. By breaking through, letting go, and as advised by the Beatles and the Disney movie *Frozen*, "let it be" and "let it go," you will open the door to abundance, because you free up all the energy trapped in those limiting beliefs—energy you need to create prosperity in your life.

Too often, we hang onto those mental obstacles or mental issues. For example, guilt is a killer. Resentment is another destroyer. We give them so much prominence and importance in our lives, but they are only feelings. That's all. They are just feelings that we're carrying that are holding us down. You've got to clear that broken relationship, clear off that business that didn't work, clear away negative thoughts and beliefs, and just throw out the anger, resentment, and guilt that have built a brick wall between you and your ability to move past them. They are blocking the things that you want, so why would you want to hang onto them?

Letting go sometimes means giving up the need to be right. It doesn't matter if you're right. What would you rather be, dead and right, or alive? You can be dead right or you can be alive. And dead doesn't necessarily mean six feet under. Dead could just mean going through life in a miserable state, which, to me, is not living - it's existing, and miserably at that.

Each of us has attitudes, underlying beliefs, and assumptions that limit abundance and prosperity. We might have grown up with them, been willed them by society or our family, or we adopted them from the people around us. Just because we have them, there is no requirement that we need to hang onto them. Our limiting beliefs might be inherited from our parents. That doesn't mean that we have to carry them throughout life. Women might have beliefs about men, and men might have beliefs about women. We all have limiting beliefs and conversations—internal conversations in our own minds that pop up to remind us what we can't do, can't have, and can't be. In order to have what we want, be what we want, and do what we want, we must clear these beliefs.

Clearing is also not just an emotional catharsis or clearing of limiting beliefs; clearing is cleaning up your environment and letting go of excess baggage. Think about the cable television series *Hoarders* – these are people who can't let go of anything. Their external environment exemplifies what is going on for them internally, as well. Clearing is about removing clutter and items from your life that weigh you down and no longer add value. Clearing is cleaning your house of old wares, cleaning your closet of old clothes, etc. It's getting rid of what no longer serves you or represents the life you want.

Clearing is very important. It might be with another person—forgiving and letting go, clearing the air, or even walking away from a relationship. It doesn't have to be with another person at all. Clearing could also be between you and the demons and negativity in your mind. Yes, we are often our biggest obstacle. Are you upset or angry? Are you insecure? Do you have money or success beliefs that are holding you back? Do you think you're not worthy or capable? Clear it—find the energy to let it go so you can fully and finally move forward.

I have friends who go to the beach to do this. They love the ocean, and it's their clearing place. They bring a symbol that represents the past and throw it into the ocean, letting the water take it far away where it will remain forever lost at sea.

We hang onto feelings, beliefs, doubts, and relationships. I have girlfriends, for example, who are still mad at their ex-boyfriend about something that happened six years ago. I have friends who are upset at a business partner who ripped them off ten years ago. As long as they hold onto that, it will stand in their way on their journey to abundance and prosperity.

The Process of Clearing With Others

How does someone clear with someone else? Always come from a responsible place. Say, "I want you to know how important you are to me, and it's important that our relationship is always transparent and honest. I want to be honest with you. There are certain things that are in my way with you, and I'd like to move past them. Do I have permission to clear with you?"

You've got to create the permission. It's up to you to establish the relationship. "You're important to me." If the person wasn't important to you, you wouldn't want to clear with them, so establish how important the person is and communicate what you need to communicate from a responsible place.

Clearing does not mean to dump on the person. Clearing isn't, "You're a jerk—look what you did to me!" No, it's, "I want you to know that I found myself getting upset because of this, this, and this, and my request is that from this point forward…" and complete it with your request. It's communicating the upset and then communicating the request. The person can either accept it or reject it, and you can choose to accept whether that person will be in your life or not. When it comes down to it, clearing is really not about the other person. Clearing is about you. It's about you clearing your energy.

I firmly believe that it's not necessary to be with the other person in order to clear with them. There's no need for a face-to-face or heart-to-heart, because if you're willing to take responsibility for your own emotions and feelings, then it's not about the other person, it's about you. You can clear without them by just making a mental commitment with yourself to move past your hurt, anger, or guilt and move forward.

The Process of Clearing with Ourselves

Just as clearing with others is important in building a mindset of abundance and prosperity, it's important to clear with yourself – clear yourself of beliefs that no longer serve you and limit all areas of your life. Our limiting beliefs are our internal GPS system. People think they need to see it to believe it, but I think that's backwards: if we believe it, we'll see it!

For example, some people have a belief that they don't deserve or cannot have money. One individual told me he had a belief that money is only intended and accessible by the top two percent. Wow! What a limiting belief. Quick! Identify it and throw it away. Clear it from your mind because it's like a cancer in your wallet and bank account, stopping you from attaining the wealth and freedom of financial independence and security you deserve.

Our beliefs don't only affect our bank accounts, they also affect our health. I've known people to turn their health around by clearing their beliefs. For example, one man had stage-four cancer when I met him. I'll call him Javier. He didn't allow his cancer diagnosis to define him, even though his sister had just died from cancer. He participated in my workshop and had the opportunity to confront his limiting beliefs and break through them. By clearing those limiting beliefs, he transformed his life and mindset from being a victim to being a victor. His health responded and improved drastically. Seven years later, he is still here and is cancer free. It's one of the most remarkable transformations I've ever seen.

Remember, beliefs are not facts—they are merely interpretations. All of those beliefs come from our past, and letting go of them can seem challenging or almost impossible. Clearing is not a one-time process—*it's a moment-to-moment choice.* Just because you were loving and giving last week, you aren't excused from being giving and expressing love this week. Just because you tossed a belief to the wayside last week, that doesn't mean you might not readopt it next week. The way we act and think every minute of our lives is a choice.

Make a choice right now to clear beliefs, attitudes, and any negative emotions you are harboring. When you do, it will feel like you've lifted a two-ton burden. Your life will be lighter. Your heart will be happier. And your mind will be clear to accept all of the amazing abundance that you've made room for.

Ways to Clear

Journaling is one way to clear. Write down those negative feelings and beliefs and attitudes that no longer serve you and the life you want to create. Get them out of your head and heart and onto paper, then close your notebook and don't look back. You could listen to a song and think about it and have a good cry. Really, crying works. How many people do you know who love to watch a tearjerker movie? The release feels great. Girls cry, boys cry—really, they do. Just give yourself permission to have a cathartic moment and let it out.

One of the things I recommend is that people play music, preferably gentle relaxation music. *Watermark* by Irish singer Enya is one of my favorites for those times when I'm feeling hurt. Listen to the music and feel it, while placing your hands on the part of your body where you feel pain. Some people feel pain in their stomach because they stuff everything inside and keep it there. Some people feel it in their hearts. Some people feel it in their heads.

If you're going through a painful moment in your life, just take a moment and take a deep breath in, let it out, then put your hands over your heart and think about those things in your life that hurt. Sometimes we're hanging onto people who died and haven't really fully felt their loss and haven't let it go, or we could be hanging onto broken relationships or broken dreams. Breathe in, hold onto your feelings for just a moment, then exhale and let it leave your body. It's a beautiful process to just clear.

Guilt is another limiting and negative belief. We beat ourselves up all of the time for things we regret, things we've done, and things we've said. Our past can be our biggest enemy. We hang onto those things we haven't forgiven or let go of. We're the kings of beating ourselves up and the queens of judgment—of ourselves, as well as others. Forgive yourself, let it go, acknowledge the beliefs, and then dissolve them.

If you're sincere and you really want to forgive, release your guilt, and let go of your doubts, negativity, and insecurities, you'll feel your load lighten and your heart lift. You'll make room for what you want, not what you don't want, in life.

Haven't you been angry long enough? Isn't it about time you forgive yourself and stop beating yourself up for things you cannot change? The past is the past. You have the power to let it go. Clear it. Get over it. And then move on.

The Value of Clearing

There is a value to clearing. It's different for each person and belief. Freedom was my greatest value. I followed this process with a past relationship, and now we're closer than ever before. At first, there was fear, but now we can be friends because we both cleared and were coming from a responsible place. Now, we can connect and have discovered an even better relationship than ever before. If we hadn't cleared, we would have both missed out on that gift.

When I cleared, it was coming from a place of gratitude. "I'm so grateful for you and our experience and our relationship, but there are things that really weren't working for me, and I wanted to express it." It was not coming from a defensive or guarded place, but rather an open and loving one. It is that energy that really makes the difference. Be positive and grateful—yes, again we see that word—for what was and what can be, turning a negative belief or attitude into a positive emotion or feeling. To me, that's better than carrying a two-ton building filled with bitterness and anger any day.

Forgiveness is the biggest way to clear and let go of anything. This is truly the key to being free. In one training, a woman shared her story—I'll call her Sara. Sara shared how a drunk driver killed her only son as he was walking to his girlfriend's house. His name was Peter; he was 18 years old and was home from college. The drunk driver's car jumped off the road onto the sidewalk and instantly killed him. Sara was heartbroken and filled with rage, especially when she found out that the driver had ten prior drunk driving convictions. Her anger and resentment was so intense that she developed cancer all over her body. Then one day, it occurred to her, "If I don't forgive the drunk driver, he will kill me, too." As part of the clearing process, she scheduled a face-to-face meeting with him in prison, and she cleared everything she was feeling until there was nothing left to say. She made the choice to forgive him. After that meeting, and in a subsequent turn of events, Sara ended up adopting this man's children, because he was sentenced to life in jail. Then, her cancer went into remission. This was ten years ago, and to this day she is cancer free.

Forgiveness is a choice to let go. This is not about the other person, or who is right; it's about choosing to have your power. So forgive everyone, especially yourself.

PRACTICE LETTING GO

Make a list of all the limiting beliefs you have that come to mind in the following areas. Once you have the list, replace each word with a positive belief. For example, replace "money is difficult" with "money is easy," replace "relationships never last" with "relationships always last," and replace "it's hard to lose weight" with "I lose weight easily."

MONEY:

RELATIONSHIP:

HEALTH:

#2 Make a list of the people you choose to forgive and what you choose to forgive them for.

Example: I forgive *my father* for *abandoning me.*

Now, your turn:

I forgive _____

for _____ .

I forgive _____

for _____ .

I forgive _____

for _____ .

I forgive _____

for _____ .

I forgive _____

for _____ .

Make a list of the things you choose to forgive yourself for.

Example: I forgive myself for being so hard on myself all of the time.

Now it's your turn:

I forgive myself for:

_____.

I forgive myself for:

_____.

I forgive myself for:

_____.

I forgive myself for:

_____.

I forgive myself for:

_____.

TWEET THIS:
*"The only way to move forward is to let go
and complete the past."*
#TransformYourLife @ChrisMotivador

"When I forgive, I am free."
#TransformYourLife @ChrisMotivador

Chapter Four

PRINCIPLE 3:
INTEGRITY

"Integrity is choosing your thoughts and actions based on your values and principles."

– Chris Lee

T HE THIRD PRINCIPLE of abundance and properity is integrity. It is honesty, wholeness, and being true to yourself. It is operating from your values and principles. Integrity is keeping your word to yourself and others. To build integrity, you can clean up broken agreements, incomplete actions, and withheld communications.

Now that we have the formal definition out of the way, let's talk about integrity. We are the first ones to break our promises to ourselves. We might have a schedule and break it. We might make arrangements or promises to others and not follow through. Whatever the situation is, it's time to clean it up and put a stop to it if we want a life of abundance and prosperity.

The undeniable thing about integrity is that it is one area where we cannot fool ourselves. We are either in integrity or out of integrity. We either act in such a way that we are upstanding or we act in such a way that we're not trustworthy. There are no shortcuts. There are no "get-rich-quick" schemes. Integrity is about doing your homework. It's about being somebody who keeps their word, honors their agreements, and operates from an ethical principled place. When you come from principles, values, and an ethical place, you create wholeness and credibility.

When you're out of agreement and integrity, your abundance is hindered because your energy is wasted and absorbed in the process of covering up, lying, and making excuses to cover up your tracks. You've heard the stories about people who have to work so hard to stay on top of their lies. One lie leads to another lie; one excuse leads to another. Any politicians or celebrities come to mind? For example, Bill Clinton and the whole Monica Lewinsky scandal. Before long, they're spending more time covering up for themselves than it would have taken to be forthright and honest and make good on their word. When we break our word and cover it up, we lose self-worth with ourselves and credibility with others.

For example, during a training, I noticed a guy – I'll call him John—who seemed extremely shut down and angry, and he was trying to convince the whole group that he didn't need to be there. I knew there was something off with his integrity. The other participants around him noticed, as well. The only one who didn't know was him – he was convinced he was perfect and didn't need to be there. As I coached him, I uncovered that he had been cheating on his wife for 12 years. As he owned up to it, and owned that he was out of integrity, his whole face changed. He became softer, open, and loving. By owning that he was out of integrity, he got his authentic self back. He made a commitment to be honest with all the parties involved. It just shows that once you address the lack of integrity in your life and come clean, it frees you up. At the end of the day, we all hide something or have guilty pleasures.

For those of you who struggle with integrity, it will be a lifelong stretch. It's not just about telling the truth—it's about being honest in other ways. It's telling people how you feel. It's about not telling people what they want to hear. Integrity is learning how to say no when you need to and how to say yes when you want to.

Do you owe people money and are avoiding them? Don't avoid them or the agreement. Have the courage to admit that you owe the money but that you don't have it right now, then make a plan to take care of it and be in integrity. You'll earn respect from two people—yourself and the person to whom you owe money.

Integrity requires two things: responsibility and response. I call it being response-able—a term I lovingly use to identify areas where we are not in integrity and not responsibly responding to it.

Being in integrity means having a principle-driven life, one with values. Everyone has values, things that are important to them that guide their lives. Take a moment to define your top ten core principles and values. What ten core principles and values are you committed to living from this point forward? Think about it and at the end of this chapter, you will have an opportunity to write them down.

Credibility is about trust and relationships. When you honor your agreements, when you keep your word, when you have ethics and operate from that platform, you create abundance and prosperity. See how it works? There's nothing that will damage your self-worth more than breaking your word (to yourself or to others), breaking agreements, lying, cheating, stealing, ripping people off, and looking for the loophole in the system so you can take advantage of it. Remember, you will always pay for everything you do in life—either you'll pay now or pay later. Like they say, you can run, but you cannot hide, especially from yourself.

Pay up now. Clear your debts to lenders, relatives, coworkers, or society. Start with a clean slate and a zero balance. Make good on your promises, pay your bills, and right your wrongs. Turn deceit into honesty and half-heartedness into sincerity. When you do, you're going to like the way you feel, and your value and self-worth will skyrocket as a result.

With your word, you have three options: you can a) keep it, b) break it, or c) renegotiate it. The only one not acceptable is to break it. When you do break it, you get to own up to it, take responsibility, and clean it up. If you choose to renegotiate your word, you must do it before your agreed time. For example, if your meeting was at 12:00 noon, you don't renegotiate at 12:01. You would renegotiate before 12:00 noon. In order for renegotiation to work, it must work for both parties and both must agree. Otherwise, it was a forced negotiation, which once again puts you out of integrity.

How to Practice Integrity:

If you want true abundance in your life, you've got to come from a place of integrity. That means cleaning up broken agreements. If you have a trail of broken agreements, clean them up. Use words like, "I'm sorry, I blew it, my bad, I acknowledge I broke the agreement, my commitment is ..." Own up to it, rather than hiding from it.

Do you have debts to pay? A garage to organize? Unfinished business or broken promises? Pay them. Organize your stuff. Finish your business. And make good on your word. A man's word used to be as good as his money. Put value back in your agreements. Get rid of the dark shadows that are hanging over you. Embrace what's hanging over you and own up to it.

The Value of Integrity:

A lot of times when we put money as the focal point of our lives, we find that money comes and then it goes. Relationships come and go. Businesses and jobs come and go. But when you put your principles at the center of your life, then you're whole and complete and can attract that. That is an abundant state.

It becomes even more abundant when your principles are in integrity and when you are in integrity with your principles. Then you'll know you're always acting and operating from an ethical place that is worthy of respect, trust, and admiration. Your principles will never let you down.

PRACTICE INTEGRITY

In the following exercise, I recommend you make a list of your top ten principles and values. If you were to pick ten principles and values that define you, what would they be? Would they be integrity, honesty, honor, or compassion? These principles can be anything; they don't have to be personality traits or ways of being. They can be spiritual or religious. There is no right, no wrong, and no grade, just an awareness of the principles that define you.

It's important to be aware of your defining principles. Sometimes these are things we forget. For that reason, I think it is valuable to write them down. Write them down and have fun with it. Decorate it and frame it, making it bold, beautiful, striking, or energetic. Mold it into something that leads you.

My top ten principles and values are:

1. _____

2. _____

3. _____

4. _____

5. _____

6. _____

7. _____

8. _____

9. _____

10. _____

In order to move forward, we must complete our past. This provides the energy, vitality, and open space for extraordinary abundance. List any incompletions or areas where you are out of integrity in the areas below and the actions you will take to move forward.

MONEY:

In the area of money, select from these categories and complete the following section.

1. Name of person or companies I owe money to:

   Example: I owe Wells Fargo Home Mortgage $2,500. Will be paid by Day, Month, Year.

   Now, it's your turn:

   I owe (Name) _____ $_____.
   Will be paid by _____

   I owe (Name) _____ $_____.
   Will be paid by _____

   I owe (Name) _____ $_____.
   Will be paid by _____

   I owe (Name) _____ $_____.
   Will be paid by _____

   I owe (Name) _____ $_____.
   Will be paid by _____

2. People or companies that owe me money.

   (Name) _____ owes me
   $_____.
   Will be paid by _____

   (Name) _____ owes me
   $_____.
   Will be paid by _____

   (Name) _____ owes me
   $_____.
   Will be paid by _____

Name) _____ owes me
$_____.
Will be paid by _____

Name) _____ owes me
$_____.
Will be paid by _____

RELATIONSHIPS

In the area of relationships, complete the following. As an example: What I have not communicated to *my mother* is "I love you." This will be completed by March 1 (date).

What I have NOT communicated to _____ is _____. This will be completed by _____ (date).

What I have NOT communicated to _____ is _____. This will be completed by _____ (date).

What I have NOT communicated to _____ is _____. This will be completed by _____ (date).

What I have NOT communicated to _____ is _____. This will be completed by _____ (date).

Pick an area of your life where you feel you are incomplete or out of integrity and write what needs to happen and by when:

Health:
What _____ by when _____

Relationships:
What _____ by when _____

Finances:
What _____ by when _____

Career:
What _____ by when _____

Education:
What _____ by when _____

Spirituality:
What _____ by when _____

Projects:
What _____ by when _____

TWEET THIS:
"When I live life from my values and principles,
I become unstoppable."
#TransformYourLife @ChrisMotivador

Chapter Five

PRINCIPLE 4:
VISUALIZATION

"Whatever you hold in your mind on a consistent basis is
exactly what you will experience in your life."
                                        – Anthony Robbins

THE FOURTH PRINCIPLE of abundance and
prosperity is visualization. The reality is, if you have
a goal or a vision, pushing for it will push it away. I've
never chased money; it has come after me. I don't chase
success; it is the result of who I am, and I attract it. When
you "be" it and live it, you will attract it.

Thus far, we've seen some of the barriers that lie
between you and abundance. It is your internal negative
conversations that cause scarcity, which comes from your
belief systems. You have to learn to practice abundance
and not pay attention to these unwelcome voices that
go off in your ear. Your principles and values will never
let you down, but you can count on the fact that those
limiting beliefs will.

Visualization is forming a clear mental picture of
the result you *do* want in its complete form, with the
intention that it will manifest in reality. It evolves out of
the creative stage of choosing your own goals.

Visualization sharpens and clarifies your goals into
a specific form and energizes them. The deeper it is in

your consciousness, the more effective the visualization will be.

Everything positive that has occurred in my life came out of a vision. You might call it a goal, a desire, or a daydream. Regardless of the terminology, visualization is actually seeing the complete result before it arrives. It's a bit like having a crystal ball, without the mystery or mystical powers surrounding it. That's because you are in total control and have exclusive power over your visualizations. You need nothing more than an intention and an imagination that lets you dream BIG.

When you visualize, it's important to be specific and able to adjust your choices as you move toward what you want. This means not being a hostage to your vision. Your vision should never feel like a burden or a have-to. You want your visions to be a joyful experience, not the deadweight of a monkey on your back.

Many people resist visualization because of fear, or they feel like they are wasting their time, or don't have the capacity to deliver on it. Once again, it's the negative voice in our head that sabotage our visions and results. If we were to visualize our future from a loving and joyful place full of possibilities, the process of making our vision a reality is not limiting, but instead quite freeing and enjoyable. Become committed to what you visualize, but don't place so many rigid specifications to it that it creates stress. One way to do that is to look at the big picture, the end result, but not the finer details and mechanics of achieving it or how it will ultimately look. There's nothing wrong with a surprise now and then, or allowing the magic of life to unfold—trust the process. When we transform fear into faith, we begin to attract what we visualize.

Before you make a declaration or a goal, you must first visualize it. For example, I might say I want to bring my family together for a reunion. In this case, the real goal isn't about wanting to hold a reunion, but instead it's really about wanting to feel the connections and love when my family comes together.

Defining the vision is the first step. You might say that you want to make $500,000, but the number isn't really your goal—it's actually financial security and independence. Someone who has a goal to be married isn't actually looking for a legal document called a marriage certificate, but they are really seeking commitment, respect, and love. If your goal is to lose weight, what is the real goal? Health? Nutrition? Energy? Self-love? That's the goal, so it would come first, followed by the goal to lose 25 or 40 pounds. The goal is the outcome, experience, and feeling. The clearer you are in regard to the experience you want, the more likely you'll achieve your goal.

We bail on our goals because they aren't enough to motivate us to achieve them. They aren't inspiring enough to make us committed to them. Whatever it is that you have not yet accomplished, well, I'm here to tell you that you don't want it enough. If you did, you'd already have it.

I'm not going to break it to you gently. If you haven't lost weight, found your soul mate, landed that job, or discovered your pot of gold, you don't want it bad enough. How do I know that? I only have to look as far as your results. If you're still looking for what it is you say you want, you aren't inspired or committed enough to find it or make it happen.

If you're committed to the extraordinary, you have to create something that will move you forward. Physical and material results will never move you forward. If you want to move forward, you must put your vision in a spiritual, emotional context.

When I got committed to my vision, I brought my family together and experienced the love and connection I wanted. I wanted it so much I wouldn't accept no for an answer or the countless excuses that were thrown my way. When I became committed to my vision of impacting people's lives, I became a trainer. But I had to approach it in the right way. The reason I wasn't yet a trainer was because I wasn't showing up as a trainer. I had to bring alive the *results* I actually wanted. In these instances, they weren't actually a family event or a title, but instead they were the feelings I desired and my vision and desire to help others. By focusing on my vision, I was able to make my visualizations a reality. Once I had that vision and was inspired, I became unstoppable— and so can you.

What's great about visualization is that it gives you something to gravitate toward. The more clearly you visualize things, the more likely it is that you will make them happen. This isn't a sidestep, an option you can pass over or come back to later when you have more time or after a thousand and one other things don't work. There is absolutely no possibility for abundance unless you create a vision of the abundance you want.

The reason many of us fall into the same traps and repeat the same breakdowns is because we're visualizing all the things we don't want. We're visualizing how it's going to fail and how it's not going to turn out the way we want. We're allowing ourselves to visualize ourselves still struggling and not having enough money. Our vision is contrary to the results we want to create, so it is only natural that the visions that become our reality are not those that motivated us in the first place.

I always say, "Be careful what you visualize because it may come true." You've got to be very conscious of your visualization. In abundance and prosperity, it's a question of channeling it in the right direction. Always make sure your visualizations include what you want, not what you don't want.

Here is a good example. A good visualization would not be, "My vision is a life without scarcity and without pain and without suffering," because by including scarcity, pain, and suffering in your vision, you'll bring those experiences alive. Try instead, "My vision is a life of abundance, a life of health, and a life of joy." Do you see the difference? Now, you're actually putting and planting into the universe and your consciousness all of the things that you really do want.

One thing is a position; another thing is a stand. When you stand for something, you're standing for something that's positive, something you want. When you position yourself, you're positioning yourself against something, such as an attack. When you create a vision, it's important that your vision be a stand. For example, Martin Luther King, Jr. stood for equality for all. Gandhi stood for world peace. They both visualized what they wanted – not what they did not want. What is your vision for the life you want to create—for your health, your finances, your family, your children, and your business? Let's say you just opened a business. What's your vision for this budding business? Is it to create a franchise or become an international conglomerate? If so, when? What do you see that business really looking like? How will it operate? What will it stand for? Where will it be headquartered? The clearer that vision, the more likely it will become a reality.

The vision you create is all-powerful. When you visualize the right thing, based on *positive* emotions, you'll get the end result. But it comes to you faster when you keep that vision front and center, where you can see it every day. Follow along and learn how to create a vision that will bring you abundance and prosperity.

How to Create a Vision:

Visions created in a meditative state are very powerful. They transfer us from the present to a state of consciousness where we can see our fulfilled goal, and we can also fully experience it and the feelings and emotions that are attached to it. Here's an example how to visualize: Take a moment and find a quiet place. Make sure there are no distractions. Turn off your cell phone. You can be in a quiet room or in a natural setting, for example, the beach, a wooded forest, or even in your shower. Close your eyes, and take a deep breath in, and let it out.

Relax. Let your mind move forward in time. Form a mental picture of what you want. Make it clear and add details. Allow yourself to live in that vision. Feel it. Embrace it. Experience the joy, the contentment, the love, the peace, the energy, and the full breadth of the emotions that accompany your vision. Visualize yourself and the result you desire. What is your vision for your health, both mental and physical? What is your vision your relationships? What is your vision your business? What is your vision for any other areas important to you? See yourself celebrating the reality of that vision in all the areas of your life. What does it feel like? What colors do you see? What are the sounds?

The more you repeat this meditative visualization process and the deeper you embed it in your consciousness, the more effective it will be. This process sets your mind in gear to work toward not only mentally experiencing the fulfillment of your vision, but it also manifests the process of actually physically experiencing it by setting your mind in motion with the emotional attachment that will bring it to fruition.

One of the other tools I use to create a vision is called a vision map or a vision board. A vision board is a very powerful tool. It's a way to see your visualization already complete. Basically, you are creating an image right in front of you of something real, of the life that you want. How do you do that? You could get cardboard, poster board, or construction paper and create a personal billboard. On that billboard, you'll place pictures, photos, drawings, words, and replicas of the things you want.

Put a picture of yourself in the center of the vision board. Then place pictures that represent areas of your life around you, like money, health, relationships, home and family, or career.

Look through magazines. If you want to have a buff body, cut out a picture of someone who already has the body you want and place it on your board to inspire, motivate, and remind you of your goal. Some people place a picture of the bodies they want to have on their refrigerator door so they can make the right choices when they open the door. If you envision the beautiful house of your dreams and see it in a magazine, cut it out and paste it on to the board. If you dream about a beautiful woman who sensually dances salsa and find a picture of her look alike—a hot, spicy, passionate Latina—what are you waiting for? Put her picture on your vision board where you can see her every day, several times a day. Every time you gaze at and admire her, you're attracting her into your life.

If your vision is to expand your business to Latin America, then place pictures of Latin America on your vision board. If you want lots of money, then add pictures of money or write yourself a check. Better yet, date it so your vision has a timeframe to meet. For example, Jim Carrey, actor/comedian, once wrote himself a check for 10 million dollars and wrote on it, "For Acting Services Rendered." He postdated it for 10 years later and said he wouldn't stop until he could cash it. He said he kept the check to keep himself inspired. At the time, he was broke, depressed, and driving an old beat up Toyota.

Have fun with it—enjoy the process. Just don't make your vision board too cluttered—if you do, your future will be cluttered, and you don't want to create that result.

It's a great process that helps you define, create, and refine precisely what you want in any and every area of your life. Think of it as a collage of your life, the way you want it to be. Display the board in a place where you can see it every day. This vision board is a very powerful tool to attract into your life all of your dreams and goals. For those of you who are technology lovers, DreamItAlive.com is a site to create digital vision boards.

Creating the vision board will initiate the process for producing maximum results. It is important that you spend a few quiet moments looking at your vision board every day. The best times are just before you go to sleep and just after you wake up. Each time you contemplate it, you intensify the creative process.

You can accelerate the process by bringing the image of your vision board to mind from time to time throughout the day. Vision boards enable you to consciously begin to create your world the way you want it to be, instead of unconsciously allowing your conditioned responses to create it some other way. Thus, they are a valuable tool for dissolving barriers for a more abundant, fulfilling life.

There is a philosophy surrounding visualization. The more we reinforce our vision, the more aware of it we become. In the process, we actually attract it in our lives. If you've always wanted a shiny red Porsche and visualize it, by keeping that vision in front of you every day, you're likely to find that you suddenly see shiny red Porsches everywhere you go. This "coincidence," also known as the Baader-Meinhof Phenomenon, is the heightening of awareness and attraction of something you visualize and commit to creating in your life.

Imagine that you're at a car dealership and you set your admiring eyes on a Lamborghini, the car of your dreams. You stare at it longingly, wishing that someday you could actually own one. But then you go home and after a couple of days, you don't think about it too much—out of sight, out of mind, right? Well, what would happen if you saw that Lamborghini every single day? You'd probably want it even more. Your admiring gaze would turn into a drool—you can taste it, feel the supple leather, and capture the new car smell when you breathe. Now you're willing to do everything and anything to be the owner of a brand spanking new Lamborghini, and you can't get it out of your mind. That's the power of visualization; it keeps your vision forefront in your mind and desires, so you're committed to driving it in the future.

The Value of Visualization:

Visualization is a very important principle because it allows us to create not just in our minds, but right in front of us in a concrete way. Creating a vision is an effective and powerful way of creating awareness toward our declarations and goals, experiencing and connecting emotionally with them, and then attracting them into our abundant and prosperous life.

PRACTICE VISUALIZATION:

1) Now that you know how to visualize, take 15 minutes a day to visualize your vision. Another recommendation is to use music as you visualize the future that is already yours. I recommend the song "Shepherd Moon" by Enya, or any other soft instrumental music you like.

2) In addition to creating a vision board for yourself, you can create additional vision boards for areas you want to focus on. For example, as a family, you can create a family vision board, or you and your significant other can create a relationship vision board, etc. The important thing is to have fun with it and be creative. You will be surprised by the amazing results you will create. Remember, always, if you have the power to visualize it, you have the power to manifest it.

TWEET THIS:
"If you have the power to visualize it, you have the power to manifest it." #TransformYourLife

"The clearer you visualize something, the more likely it is to happen." #TransformYourLife

Chapter Six

PRINCIPLE 5:
AFFIRMATION

"It's the repetition of affirmations that lead to belief and once that belief becomes a deep conviction, things begin to happen."

– Claude M. Bristol

SO FAR, WE'VE made amazing progress in our quest for abundance and prosperity. The next principle in abundance and prosperity is affirmation. Once we have our clear vision, have manifested it on paper or a vision board, and reinforced it in our mind, the next step is to affirm it. An affirmation is declaring it to be already so, as if it was real, before it is. It's establishing a mental consciousness of what we want by putting it into words in a positive way, again as if it is already reality. In essence, you're living the future in the present.

Affirmations are words planted in our minds and in our hearts that will grow as life unfolds around us. These words are not in reaction to what is. These words are designed to create and manifest what we want for our future in the present. Do a little time traveling. Look through your lens into the future. What will you be ten years from today? Who you will be? Who will you be with? Where will you be? What will you be doing? How old will you be? What will you be feeling?

When you write your affirmation, state the environment, the experience, or the feelings. Always write it in the present tense, not in the future, or it will remain in the future. What is the environment? What is the experience? Then, what is the specific measurable result?

For example, if your goal for the future is to be in a relationship, your affirmation would be, "I am now experiencing absolute fulfillment and joy with my soul mate." See what I did? I wrote the experience and the emotion first, then the result … as if they have already happened.

That is an affirmation. It's declaring in writing the future to be what I want it to be, with the experiences and feelings that are associated with it, again, as if the future was today.

Language anchors us into reality. We're always making affirmations. For example, when we say, "This traffic is killing me," we're affirming that the traffic is, indeed, killing us. As soon as we affirm it, we're guaranteeing that the traffic isn't going to make us feel good. We're certainly not going to enjoy our commute for the next hour because we've already affirmed the outcome we will experience is going to be a dreaded one.

Every time we speak, we're making an affirmation. If you affirm that today is going to be stressful or that you're already stressed, you guessed it … hello, stress! Come on in! You can't escape it because that is the outcome and experience you've already attached to today or a particular event.

With us knowing it, all of our limiting beliefs are negative affirmations. For example, "I'm not good enough," "I'm not smart enough," "I'm not pretty enough," "I'm not talented enough," etc., are all negative affirmations— these affirmations affect everything we think, speak, feel, and create. By shifting the negative affirmations and creating positive affirmations, our lives will transform. Remember, if you believe it, you will see it.

Try this exercise: write one negative affirmation for each of the ten areas. For example, I am ugly. I am not smart, etc.:

1) I am _____
2) I am not _____
3) I am too _____
4) My body is _____
5) Men are _____
6) Women are _____
7) Love is _____
8) Relationships are _____
9) My age means _____
10) Exercising is _____

> Go back and cross out all the negative affirmations and replace them with positive affirmations. For example, "I am ugly" becomes "I am beautiful;" "I am not smart" becomes "I am brilliant," etc.

In this principle, though, I share how to use affirmations to create powerful words that open up possibilities, instead of affirmations that reinforce the things that are opposite of what we want.

In creating affirmations, make it real. Connect with it. *Feel it.* "Today, I am relaxing and marveling at the gorgeous scenery outside my oceanfront villa on the coast of St. Lucia." That'll work. Why? Well, even if you inwardly doubt your ability to buy that dream home, you'll certainly be able to believe how relaxing and beautiful it is and how much you'll enjoy being there. You're now emotionally connected to it, and when that happens, it's enough to create the mind shift that will inspire you to want it badly enough to really make it happen. In other words, you're looking for the abundance first, not the prosperity or byproduct. In this example, the abundance is the *feeling,* the villa is the byproduct or result.

Affirmations can be verbal or written. Written affirmations are powerful because they get your goal out of your head and give them life and permanency. Once that affirmation is in writing, it's real and can't be retracted. And there's another bonus, a written affirmation provides a visualization of the goal, so it serves dual duty.

Examples of Affirmations:

"I am an effective and passionate public speaker." That's a positive affirmation. Affirmations should always be positive. But let's say you really feel like you're not passionate or effective, what happens then? Can you fake it till you make it? No. But the affirmation will go to work to shift your mind and your inner beliefs and give you the confidence and passion to really become the speaker you want to be. The more you become conscious of it, the more it empowers you.

Let's say you're really horrible at managing your money. You create an affirmation that says something like, "I manage my money easily and effortlessly." The more you affirm it, the more your subconscious strives to work toward making it a reality. Affirmations are creating a statement of the things you want to be able to be effective at, even if they are things that are challenging to you at the moment.

It is like making a promise with yourself. Remember, what you think and what you speak creates your reality, so what you're doing is creating Kryptonite to the negativity and replacing it with an impenetrable boulder of positivity.

Affirmations aren't just point-blank statements, "I am this or that." Done. They're not effective without the verbiage that gives them life and feelings. Let's say you've had a hard time being a responsible person because you break your word all of the time. Maybe you're a victim, you have a difficult time showing love, or you have a hard time being powerful, so you would integrate words like "responsible, powerful, loving" and create different affirmations that respond to the things you need. Attach a feeling to it, stating how being responsible, loving, and powerful it makes you feel right now. It's the feeling that will connect you to that affirmation every time.

Affirmations aren't reserved for things, the stuff we accumulate in our lives. Affirmations can be about anything, especially non-tangible things like clearing, opening up, self-expression, self-esteem, happiness, integrity, wealth, money, success, relationships, and love.

Here are examples of a few affirmations I love:

It's okay for me to release my entire past. It is now complete, and I am free of it!
I am dynamically self-expressive.
It's okay for me to have fun and enjoy myself, and I do.
I keep my agreements easily and joyously.
Large sums of money, big happy financial surprises, and rich appropriate gifts come to me and totally satisfy me in harmonious ways for my own personal use. I accept this fully.
I have an unfailing, free-flowing, and ever-expanding financial income, NOW!
I always get the most satisfying results.
I love, admire, and respect people, and they love, admire, and respect me.
I recall everything that is needed.

How to Create Affirmations:

There are all kinds of affirmations you can create for yourself. There are affirmations on public speaking and self-esteem. There are affirmations on money management and relationships. Some affirmations are about health and fitness. Spiritual affirmations are incredible. Regardless of the affirmations you choose, know that they represent a positive attitude, and when you affirm, you are turning that positive attitude into something you create for yourself.

I recommend that people create their own affirmations based on their personal goals and situations. Basically, you're speaking to the things you want to create. You don't want to word it in such a way that you're in reaction to what currently is.

For example, let's say you have a horrible backache and it's something you've been struggling with for quite some time. You're not going to say, "My back no longer hurts," because that reinforces the fact that your back hurts. A better way to word it is, "I am now enjoying a painless experience with my back," or "My back is healthy and clear." "I can move my back freely and with ease." Now you're speaking to the experience you want, not what you don't want.

Affirmations should include positive, not negative, words, such as "am, can, and will." They must proclaim positive words in the present state.

Think about the areas you need to work on and improve. Chances are you already know what they are. Which areas are challenging you right now? Maybe it's challenging for you to be expressive. Maybe it's challenging for you to be detail-oriented. Maybe it's challenging for you to trust others. Maybe it's challenging for you to be focused because you have permanent ADHD.

Now, take those challenges and create an affirmation that removes them. Put them in the past and affirm a life without them and how that makes you feel. Feels good, doesn't it?

Writing your own affirmations is very simple. Make sure they are in the present tense, not the past or the future. Be positive and put your creative energy toward the positive result. Another tip is to maintain the attitude that you're creating something new, not old. Avoid falling into the "having to have it" mindset and focus instead on the feeling of already having it.

The Value of Affirmations:

Whatever it is that's challenging, when you create affirmations that are positive, they become a treasure map of sorts and a reminder of what you want. These positive affirmations support and inspire you. They are now more than wishes—they are promises to yourself that you become emotionally obligated to keep. Affirmations play a very important role in keeping your promises because they empower you to keep your mind focused on the future you want to create, not the present or the past you want to change.

It's your future. Affirm it.

AFFIRMATIONS

PRACTICE AFFIRMATIONS:

TWEET THIS:
"Replace negative affirmations with positive ones –
and watch your life expand."
#TransformYourLife @ChrisMotivador

Sample Affirmations:

On Happiness:

I deserve to be happy, and I am!
Happiness is a choice I make – moment to moment.
My life is a joyful, happy adventure.
I am happy.

On Self-esteem:

I am a powerful, loving, and unstoppable being, and I
love myself.
I am strong, bold, and beautiful.
I acknowledge and appreciate myself daily.
I forgive myself.

On Love:

I love freely and unconditionally.
I am surrounded by love.
I transform fear into love.

On Success:

The whole universe is behind me, backing up all my visions.
I easily manifest my visions into reality.
My vision board is manifested.
I deserve and enjoy my success.

On Integrity:

I give and easily keep my word.
I live my principles and values.
I communicate my feelings freely and effortlessly.
Everything I begin, I complete.

Write your own affirmations. Pick the areas of your life that you're committed to transforming and write an affirmation for each area. Remember, only include what you do want. Keep it positive, in the present, and short.

Then add your TOP THREE affirmations to your personal vision board.

Chapter Seven

PRINCIPLE 6:
DECLARATION

"A declaration is the beginning of turning a dream into a reality."

– Chris Lee

ONCE I HAVE my consciousness of abundance, I'm so full of abundance that I'm giving and giving! I've cleared my past, and I operate from integrity. I visualize my future, and I've created my vision board. I'm also armed with my affirmations, which are positive messages that I've written down for myself. The next step in creating this wonderful, amazing thing called abundance and prosperity is to establish what's called a declaration.

A declaration is affirming that you have what it takes to manifest your goal. A declaration is simply making a choice. A declaration is focusing on what you really want, deep in your heart, not what others want for you, but what YOU truly want. A declaration is transforming your vision that you visualized into a laser of intention. A declaration is critical because it gives you a vehicle to manifest all your visions. A declaration is also about trust—trust that the process works, trust that everything happens for a reason, and trust that the universe has the resources for you to accomplish what you want, when you want, and with whom you want. Setting goals, both short-term and long-term, is a manifestation of declaration.

A declaration is made in a surrendering manner. Be very clear about the ability of the universe to assist you. Do not force the universe to give you what you want, but proceed with the intention that it will fulfill your goal.

My limiting beliefs hate declarations, but the leader in me knows and trusts that life is full of declarations. There are no limitations. I come from a place of, "I have the power to create what I want, when I want, where I want, with whom I want. I can have it all." Then I'm ready to make a declaration.

In order to be effective, a declaration does have specific requirements. It's a goal that needs to be made in a measurable timeframe, while trusting that the resources are already there to make it happen. Stating that someday you're going to be rich or thin is not the same as saying that by January 1st of next year, you're going to save $5,000 or lose 20 pounds.

An action plan accompanies a declaration. You're making an affirmation into the world, even if you don't have a clue how it will turn out. To me, this lack of evidence takes us out of our comfort zone, which is a good thing. Actually, it's spectacular! It's living life on the edge, which is exhilarating and a life that's worth living. Trust the process.

If something is not going the way you want, declare what it is that you're committed to creating. Do you want a better relationship or improved health? Let a declaration lead you there. If you're life becomes boring or routine, listen up—you are not declaring big enough. Get out of your comfort zone! Life begins outside of your comfort zone. Stretch yourself and you'll be surprised at the results.

When making a declaration, it is very important that you are not in reaction to what is happening that you want to change. Declarations are similar to affirmations—you are declaring something in the future. The difference is considerable. An affirmation is a statement. A declaration is a goal, one that's measurable and has a firm deadline.

Goals take life and turn it into an enjoyable game. It's a unique road map that you create, with all the stops, scenery, and attractions along the way. Concrete goals will take you from one point to another, without unnecessary detours and layovers.

Making a goal is about trusting that I'm going to make my best effort to get to that goal, but I don't need to be consumed by it. Again, I trust the process; I don't chase it. Sometimes people get so consumed by their goals that they actually push their goals away. If I have to have that relationship and I show up on a date with that need, what's going to happen? My date is likely to reject my feelings, thinking they don't want to be with someone who is so needy.

What about a job? Maybe you're an actor going to a casting audition, and in your mind you're saying, *I just have to get this part. I just have to ace this audition and land the role.* You're sweating bullets and you're nervous; your voice is cracking and you can't communicate clearly.

What's likely to happen? The casting director is going to push you away. "You know what? You're not the candidate for us." Declaring is never an absolute I-can't-live-without-it, this-has-absolutely-got-to-happen desperate plea. It's about creating and declaring from a joyful, abundant place and trusting that the universe will manifest the results you want.

It also doesn't mean to be apathetic or resigned or assuming the attitude that whatever happens, happens. No! Make it happen, go for it! But don't be attached to it and trust the process. Remember, the universe has the resources to make it happen. Trust it—you'll be surprised.

How to Declare Goals:

"I declare that X will happen by Y."

A declaration is specific and measurable. Even if goals are expansive and general, you can make them specific, breaking them down into bite-size nuggets that are detailed. State what you are going to accomplish in life and by when. Your declaration can be about health, family, finances, love, relationships, or your career.

When you declare goals, I suggest that you write them down. Writing them down is very important. Just like with affirmations, I recommend that you start with the future from the present. Imagine 10 years into the future. Now, ask yourself these questions: "In 10 years, how old will I be? What are the 10 goals I want to have accomplished by then?"

I recommend that people actually transfer that to paper. "Today is [the future date]. I am [age] and here are the top 10 goals I have accomplished." Again, write them down as if they have already happened. Then break that down from 10 years to 5 years, to 1 year, to 1 month, and to 1 week. In this way, you'll become aware in the next week that you're actually creating the next 10 years and you're making progress!

Ten years will come, no matter what. In fact, it's coming sooner than you think. When it arrives, you'll look back and think the time literally flew. Isn't time really an illusion? It's very important to be in the consciousness of the future now. After all, our present reality is going to be a mere memory in ten years.

I remember when the year 2000 seemed so very far away, and when we got to the year 2000, we all thought, "Wow, that came fast!" It's just amazing. Time flies, and life flies by right with it. Before you know it, we're looking at what's next as we roll through the years.

By using declarations, you're taking responsibility for the future outcomes in your life. In other words, you're not spinning your wheels and leaving your life to chance. You're creating goals and declaring them from that point in the future. Then everything you do today is working toward it with the full, unblemished trust that the universe has your back.

An incredible example of somebody who wrote a declaration and benefitted from its power is actor Jim Carrey. Jim Carrey wrote himself a check for ten million dollars. Now, that's a lofty goal. The year was 1985. At that time, he was renting an apartment and barely able to pay his bills. Broke and depressed, he drove his beat up Toyota up to Hollywood Hills and declared that he wasn't going to give up. He had no fortune or fame and no real prospects for acquiring either one. But he wrote himself a check for ten million dollars and said, "I'm not stopping until I can cash this check." He visualized his future. He affirmed it, and he declared it. And he gave it a date, postdating the check for ten years later. He then put that check in his wallet. That check and declaration did manifest ten million dollars. In fact, it manifested more than ten million—proof that there is nothing wrong with declaring BIG!

There's nothing wrong with living in the present, but having a 10-year game plan and goals for the next 10 years makes the present more enjoyable, because what you're doing now creates the future. Too often, we don't realize that our actions today are going to create tomorrow. Jim Carrey knew that, too. He knew that his declaration alone wasn't enough, that he'd have to do something to help make it happen. That something was acting. On the notation line on the check, he referenced that, writing, "For acting services rendered."

I live in the moment, but I also have my game plan very clear because it's about being effective. If I want abundance and prosperity, these are the tools that are going to bring me to that. Walt Disney said it best. "If you can dream it, you can achieve it."

However, if there is no intention to it, it won't happen. You must be committed to it and have the certainty of knowing that it absolutely will happen.

The Value of Declarations:

Declarations take affirmations one step further. They take a statement of something that will be in the future and partner it with goals, then declaring that it will be so, even if there is no evidence to support the fact. Declarations are created and manifested in trust. Trust the universe. Trust that you have every resource you'll possibly need to make your declaration a reality. With positive intentions, the increased value you'll receive from declaring your goals is manifestation of your desires, even if they are ten-million-dollar dreams.

PRACTICE DECLARATIONS BY SETTING GOALS

Make sure your goals line up with your vision. Be specific and give them a deadline. Write why the goal is important to you. In the following space, take the time to write down the top five goals you will accomplish by the time established. Write them down as if you have already accomplished them. For example, "I am now living in my ocean front home surrounded by my wife/husband, and # of children. I am feeling loved, fulfilled, and blessed. My life is full of joy."

My goals for the next ten years are:

1. _____

2. _____

3. _____

4. _____

5. _____

My goals for the next five years are:

1. _____

2. _____

3. _____

4. _____

5. _____

My goals for the next year are:

1. _____

2. _____

3. _____

4. _____

5. _____

My goals for the next month are:

1. _____

2. _____

3. _____

4. _____

5. _____

TWEET THIS:
"When I declare what I want, the universe conspires."
#TransformYourLife @ChrisMotivador

Chapter Eight

PRINCIPLE 7:
PERSISTENCE

"In the confrontation between the stream and the rock, the stream always wins, not through strength, but through persistence."

— H. Jackson Brown

THE SEVENTH PRINCIPLE of abundance and prosperity is persistence. What is persistence, you ask? Persistent means not being a quitter. Persistence is the continuation of choosing your goal. As I continue to choose the goal over and over and over, that allows me to be persistent. Unfortunately, this principle is often overlooked.

For example, I was once 20 pounds heavier than I am today. I'm 6'2" and carry my weight well, but I was aware that I had gained a few and was getting overweight. So I made a goal and I visualized weighing a certain amount. Along the way, though, I had to keep choosing my goal, which took persistence. I had to choose that goal every time I didn't feel exercising or working out. I had to choose that goal when I had to sacrifice a double cheeseburger and fries and eat a salad instead. I had to choose that goal every time I was tempted or discouraged with the needle on the scale.

Persistence is being relentless, stating your goal and intentions are not negotiable, even when there are obstacles, challenges, or other temptations that are calling you in a different direction.

Persistence will assist you in moving through barriers that are in the way of you achieving your goal. If your goal is to be healthy and physically fit, but you find yourself too sore and tired to hit the gym and work out, persistence is the principle that will push you through potential breakdowns.

Persisting is when I repeatedly remind myself, "This is my goal." Sometimes we think it's just about choosing a goal once, but that's why we often don't create the reality we want. We don't want it badly enough—we're not persistent. Weight loss isn't a one-thought or one-wish goal that you throw out to the universe and, whoosh, it happens and the pounds melt away. It takes persistence.

Marriage requires persistence. You make a declaration on your wedding day and choose this life that you want to lead, but if you don't choose that life tomorrow, next year, or ten years from now, the marriage you wanted to create might not be your reality.

Do whatever it takes, not just today, but tomorrow, next week, and next year. It doesn't matter how you feel. It doesn't matter if you're in the mood. It doesn't matter if you like or don't like what you're doing. It doesn't matter if every muscle in your body feels like it has been run over by a Mack truck. Don't quit. Stop making excuses. Push through the pain. The important thing is you've got to keep your eye on your vision and be committed to that vision, beyond how you feel. Like I said before, you have to want it *enough*.

Most of us back out of goals because we just don't feel like keeping them anymore. To all those people who are overweight, I hate to say it, but you're overweight because you don't feel like losing weight. Those of you who are broke and don't have money and abundance, I going to come right out and tell you the truth: the reason you don't have money is not because of the economy, rotten luck, or a lack of opportunities, but because you haven't been persistent about it. You don't want it enough.

My premise is that every human being has the power to create the life that they want. If they're not creating it, there's something that is not working. They're not committed enough. They're not persistent and willing to do anything and everything to make it happen. They're making excuses, not progress.

When I commit to my vision in a persistent way, the circumstances that threaten to impede my progress disappear. The conversations and excuses go away. More than two decades ago, I decided I would no longer be manipulated by my body and my brain, or by time, money, fear, or other circumstances. Today, I no longer consult how I feel before doing something. I don't consult my checkbook or my calendar before committing to anything. I don't consult my moods or my opinions. I do, however, consult my vision. If it aligns with my vision, I'm a maniac on a mission. Whatever comes my way, bring it! I'm ready to overcome it.

Every goal you might have is possible … if you are persistent. The difference between a leader and a wannabe isn't their visions. It's that the leader is persistent, but the wannabe has an excuse.

Say goodbye to excuses and hello to results. My life is full of results the minute I give up the stories. Give up your stories. Give up your excuses. Be on a mission and let nothing or no one get in your way.

How to Implement Persistence:

Jim Carrey didn't write himself a check and then forget about it. He didn't just go through his life day to day, doing nothing at all toward earning the money he was attempting to manifest. He worked toward it. He reminded himself of his goal every day. The check was in his wallet, which admittedly didn't contain too much of anything else, so he saw that check frequently. He chose the goal every time he saw the check. And then he set out to earn part of that ten million dollars every chance he could.

How can you implement persistence? On a regular basis, revisit your vision, affirmation, and declaration. Whether it's the first thing you do in the morning or the very last thing you do before your head hits the pillow at night, revisit your intention and reinforce it in your consciousness.

Look back on the goals you've made in the past. How many have you actually accomplished? How many have fallen to the wayside? How many did you give up on because it required too much time, work, effort, or pain?

Learn from your past. Stop making excuses. Silence that conversation in your mind that tells you it's okay to wait another day. Stifle that voice that says, "Not today. I don't wanna. I can't. I have something better to do." Tell it to shut up and go away. That voice is your enemy. It's trying to sabotage the manifestation of your goals. And I'm here to tell you, that voice is more persistent than you are right now. That voice won't go away until you make it go away.

How? Ignore it. Reinforce your desire and your goal. Be persistent, push through and move forward. Do one thing toward your goal that will defy and despise the voice that's trying to keep you in your comfort zone. You're bigger than your doubts, fears, pains, and excuses. You know what they're capable of; they've shown you many times. It's time to learn what you're capable of when you want something enough that you're committed to it, not just when you affirm and declare it, but each and every day. That's the kind of get-out-of-my-way persistence that creates results, not excuses.

The Value of Persistence:

You may not have the reality you want today. You probably won't have it tomorrow. But one thing is for sure, you'll never have it if you aren't clear and persistent toward your intentions. Spinning wheels are like brakes—neither one makes any progress. Stop spinning your wheels and creating a hole that only gets deeper and deeper. You've got to start somewhere, so just get moving. With each day, it gets easier to gain momentum and make major headway toward the manifestation of your goal.

You can only make progress if you're dedicated and committed. Be persistent. Like a salesman who won't take no for an answer, hound yourself until you wear out every excuse and the only answer left is Yes! Yes, today I'm going to do A, B, and C. With persistence, you'll get there and find that getting to X, Y, and Z wasn't as hard as it looked.

When you give up, you get in your own way. You hit a roadblock, a dead end. When you get going, you find a way. You blaze a path straight through the excuses, the procrastination, the pain, weariness, doubts, and uncertainties. That's the value of persistence on the road to abundance and prosperity.

PRACTICE PERSISTENCE

Persistence is not quitting, no matter what. Most people bail when there is a breakdown or because they don't feel like keeping their goals anymore. In order to accomplish your goals, you need to give up your feelings and excuses. Have your vision guide you, not your circumstances. Turn any breakdowns into breakthroughs on the road toward your goals.

6 Steps to Turn Breakdown of Your Goals into Breakthrough

For example, sample goals that turned into breakdowns:

- I declared that I would lose 10 pounds, and instead I gained 15 pounds.
- I declared that I would sell $10,000 of services in my business, instead I sold $3,000.
- I declared that I would spend more time with my family, and I did not.
- I declared balance in my life, and instead created chaos.

What most people do when they have these breakdowns is A) Cover them up and pretend nothing happened, B) Beat themselves up by feeling bad and guilty or blaming somebody else, or C) Come up with a great excuse for not completing the declaration. The problem with this strategy is that it guarantees failure and a state of insanity, which, according to Einstein, is completing the same thing over and over and expecting a different result. This happens to our New Year's resolutions; we make them, and within weeks we have already broken them. Then the next year, we make the same resolutions again. To transform this, I have created the following six steps.

1) Acknowledge the breakdown in a positive way and add the word "YES!" (Why positive? Because either way I need to solve the breakdown, and every breakdown is a blessing in disguise if we learn from them.)
Example: I promised to lose 10 pounds, and instead I gained 15. YES!

2) Take responsibility. (Stop blaming others—remember you are the source.) Identify what was missing from you, what you could have done differently, and what lesson you can learn from this.
Example: What was missing from me was discipline, persistence, and surrounding myself with people who support my declaration. Lesson learned: I cannot allow my cravings to dominate me.

3) Forgive. (Self, others, universe) You need that energy to accomplish your declaration.

Example: I forgive myself, and I forgive everyone who encouraged me to break my diet.

4) Make a new commitment. (So what, now what? It's a new moment.) What's your new declaration, and by when?
Example: My new declaration is to lose 25 pounds by X date.

5) Take action with urgency. (Create an action plan and execute.)
Example: My new action plan is X diet, X exercise daily, maintain a calorie log, and hire a personal trainer.

6) See your results. (When accomplished, celebrate. If you don't accomplish, go back to step 1.)
Example: When I hit my target, I get to celebrate, for example, buy an outfit in my new size or take myself on exotic trip. If not, go back to Step 1, and start over again.

Accomplishing our declarations requires major persistence, and it may take repeating these steps over and over until you get it done. Now it's your turn: Think of a goal you have not achieved yet, and apply the six steps to that goal.

1. Acknowledge the breakdown in a positive way and add the word "YES!"
2. Take responsibility.
3. Forgive.

4. Make a new commitment.
5. Take action with urgency.
6. See your results.

TWEET THIS:
"Never give up on your dreams."
#TransformYourLife @ChrisMotivador

Chapter Nine

PRINCIPLE 8: SURRENDERING

"Surrender to what is. Let go of what was. Have Faith in what will be."

– Sonia Ricotti

THE PRINCIPLES OF abundance and prosperity are already working for you. Look at the progress and steps you've taken to open yourself up to the universe and attract what you want!

The eighth principle that will support you along the way is surrendering, versus being attached and resistant. Wait a minute. I just told you that you had to be persistent, like a maniac on a mission. You have to be relentless and show up at every turn, regardless if your inner voices and conversations try to persuade you otherwise. How is it possible to be that persistent and not be attached to your goal? The way to do that is to keep choosing the goal with the timeline that you've set for yourself. It's reminiscent of the saying, "It's not over until the fat lady sings." Don't give up, no matter what. With this principle, you keep the faith and your dream alive.

Once I hit that platform or timeline, I've reached a point where I need to either make a new goal, shift the goal, or negotiate the goal, but I need to surrender and be unattached when doing so.

If I choose a goal, I'm not choosing the goal in order to be somebody. In other words, the goal isn't me; we are not joined at the hip and inseparable. I have an identity and self-worth outside of and regardless of that goal. Who I am is bigger than any result. Most people attach their self-worth to their net worth. When we become attached to our results, we then have to have the result. When we have to *have* something, we automatically energize the opposite. Nobody wants to date someone who is desperate. Nobody is going to hire somebody who shows up needy. For example, I had a friend, we will call her Lisa, that was beautiful, intelligent, and all around an extraordinary human being. She owned her own business and had a beautiful home and lots of great friends. From the outside, she appeared to be successful. As I got to know her, and started to coach her, I noticed something interesting – every relationship she started would end within months. This baffled me until I uncovered the source of this breakdown of her life. I spoke to one of the guys she dated, and here's what he said to me: "When I first met Lisa, she was a dream come true. As I started dating her, she became a nightmare. After the first date, she was already talking about moving in together and marriage. It was almost like she had the wedding dress in the trunk of her car. Needless to say, this freaked me out, and I ran." Once I found out this information, I knew exactly how to coach my friend Lisa. Her issue was being attached to the relationship, marriage, etc. By being attached to all that, she lost sight of what a real relationship is … which is connection, love, trusting the process, and allowing the magic of the relationship to unfold. When we don't trust the process and try to manipulate and control the outcomes, we push our goal further and further away. I coached Lisa on this very principle: Surrender, trust yourself, and trust the process. I coached her to ...

Transform fear into faith.

Fear is the expectation that things are going to turn out in a negative way. Faith is the expectation that things are going to turn out in a positive way. Lisa began to apply this coaching in her life, and not only did every area of her life take new ground, but she began a new relationship that turned into marriage. That was ten years ago. I walked Lisa down the aisle on the day of her wedding. She surrendered to the relationship, trusted the process, and did not try to control the outcome. As a result, the magic of the relationship unfolded, leading to her dream, which was to be married. Surrendering doesn't only apply to relationships; it applies to all areas of our lives.

For example, a lot of people want to lose weight for the wrong reasons. They want to lose weight because they want to look good, and then they get attached to it. When they don't hit the goal and it doesn't look exactly like they thought it would, they beat themselves up. They feel bad, let down, and discouraged. It's like they attach their self-perception to the goal, not to themselves. That's a very negative place to come from because it cannot be corrected.

When you don't meet a goal, you've got to be willing to see beyond your results. It's important to be able to forgive yourself. "You know what? I acknowledge myself because I went for it. I was persistent, and I did whatever it took. I didn't accomplish it; I know that. I can't change that. Now, what's the lesson? What can I learn from it, because I'm still a great person, regardless of whether I hit a goal or not."

Don't hinge your self-worth on your goal. Don't pity yourself, either. Don't put yourself down and tear yourself apart when you fall short of accomplishing what you want. Forgive yourself and learn from what happened ... or didn't happen ... and use that knowledge to manifest different results the next time.

Moving forward, ask yourself, "What worked? What didn't work? What needs to be different?" Remember, you are not your goals. They do not define you; they define what you want. It's really important not to be attached in life. The minute we get attached to things, we become victims. If I become attached to having a relationship, a business, or a specific result, then I become a victim of it, versus having the vision of being in a relationship or the vision of having success in my business. I can be connected to my vision, and out of my vision, I'm committed to it.

Thomas Edison was persistent in his attempts to create the light bulb. However, he didn't always succeed. In fact, he failed. Ten thousand times! Whew! Now, that's persistence. It's also validation that he didn't attach himself to his goal or berate himself each time he didn't accomplish it. He said, "I didn't fail. I just found 10,000 ways that don't work." In other words, he learned something each and every time. With each attempt, he saw himself growing closer and closer to manifesting his vision.

What would have happened if Edison had chosen to beat himself up and bully himself with self-criticism the first time he failed? He probably wouldn't have attempted to create his vision again. Can you imagine the destruction to his self-worth if he'd put himself down and affirmed what a failure he was all 10,000 times?

I can tell you what would have happened. The world wouldn't have benefitted from his vision and his genius. He would have given up, not because he was trying to do the impossible, but because he'd convinced himself that he wasn't capable or worthy of success.

Edison wasn't a failure, and neither are you. You're bright, committed, and visionary. If for some reason your vision, affirmation, and declaration don't give birth, it's okay. Hold your head up high. You tried. Maybe you didn't get it right the first time, but now you know how to get it right the next time. That's the beauty of abundance and prosperity—we get to improve, learn, create, and recreate as often as we want to. The beauty of our life is we can keep getting back on our horse, no matter how many times we fall.

It's not the end of the world if you don't accomplish something. It is the end of the world, though, if you quit, because if you quit, that means you're giving up and hanging up your hat. You're resigning—resigning from trying and resigning from growing. You're acclaiming that this is it, folks, there isn't anything more. Don't let one letdown or disappointment prevent you from experiencing a lifetime of amazing hoorahs. When you do that, you resign from living and creating an abundant and prosperous life.

Surrender is not resigning. Surrender is flow. It's letting go of self-criticism and judgment. It's trusting that life is as it should be and everything is a blessing. Be in the flow. Be in the magic and in awe. Be in that state of consciousness where you're flowing on the ocean of life and tapping into the vibrant colors of its energy. It's the zone. That will also create the abundance and the prosperity, which are what you're really seeking.

Surrendering allows you to clear the negativity from your mind so it doesn't get in the way of your future. Once you're clear, you can focus and tap into other energies, like creativity, so you can put your attention toward attempting your goals again or attracting and manifesting something different, and possibly better, in your life. It's true that you cannot move forward if you're looking back.

Go back to clearing and surrender. Say, "I didn't succeed. Thank you." Thank the universe for the opportunity, the education, and the inspiration and fortitude to try. Don't get frozen in failure—let it go. Kiss it goodbye and throw it to the wind. Feel the release as you rejoice in being free to change your action plan or your goal altogether and plunge forward into the excitement of creating something new.

Achieving goals in a persistent and surrendering way will facilitate moving through barriers to greater personal growth, as well as creating success and achievement. Be persistent, but don't attach yourself to the goal. When you're not attached to it, you can actually move it forward with less effort. You'll find that you're more flexible with the end result and better able to adapt the details and steps you need to take to get you there.

Many times in life, we are in situations that cannot control, such as our health, how people treat us, the traffic, weather, injustice, breakdowns, and life's curveballs. If we resist those things when they happen, it makes it worse.

"What you resist persists." – C.G. Jung

By accepting and embracing these curveballs, we can use our energy to maintain our happiness and find a solution that will empower us. Remember, even when we are in a no-control situation, whether it's health, finances, or relationships, we have 100% control how we choose to see it. We can resist it, and suffer through it, or we can embrace it and see the blessing in each situation.

"Pain is mandatory, suffering is optional." – Dali Lama

PRACTICE SURRENDERING

When we allow ourselves to trust the process of life, and we surrender, we live in the flow. The flow is connecting to the universal energy. It's like being part of a big ocean; when pain and suffering appear in our lives, we see them as blessings. By not resisting them, we can use that energy and redirect it in our favor. For example, in the martial arts sport of Aikido, the artist is trained to embrace his opponent's attack, versus resisting it. If he resists the attack, he will be defeated. Instead, he's trained to accept that energy and redirect it in his favor. We can do the same in our lives. Everything is energy, whether it's a relationship, health, or money. If we resist it, we push it away further. By embracing it, we can have it work in our favor.

Think of 10 things that you resist daily. For example, there are things you have to do, or people and/or situations you have to deal with. In the exercise below, fill in the situation that you resist but have to do. After each, write the feelings that come up for you as a result of the "I have tos" in your life.

Examples:
I have to *pick up my kids from school every day and sit in traffic, as if I'm their chauffeur.*
 I feel *exhausted, angry, unappreciated, stressed out.*

1. I have to _____
    I feel _____

2. I have to _____
    I feel _____

3. I have to _____
   I feel _____

4. I have to _____
   I feel _____

5. I have to _____
   I feel _____

6. I have to _____
   I feel _____

7. I have to _____
   I feel _____

8. I have to _____
   I feel _____

9. I have to _____
   I feel _____

10. I have to _____
    I feel _____

Notice all the stress and anxiety that all of those "have tos" produce in life. This is the consequence of resistance. When we resist life, we are in conflict with what is. This causes us to be in breakdown. When we surrender and embrace "what is," our anxiety and stress diminish. When we see those "have tos" as blessings, we step into surrender and experience joy and gratitude.

Now, take the same ten items from the "have to" list above and insert them in the blanks below. Then, write the feelings that come up as a result.

For example, I am blessed to *pick up my kids from school.*
I feel gratitude that I have kids and that I am healthy. I feel
appreciative of the time this allows me to spend with them.

1. I am blessed to_____
   I feel _____

2. I am blessed to_____
   I feel _____

3. I am blessed to_____
   I feel _____

4. I am blessed to_____
   I feel _____

5. I am blessed to_____
   I feel _____

6. I am blessed to_____
   I feel _____

7. I am blessed to_____
   I feel _____

8. I am blessed to_____
   I feel _____

9. I am blessed to_____
   I feel _____

10. I am blessed to_____
    I feel _____

TWEET THIS:
"Transform fear into faith."
#TransformYourLife @ChrisMotivador

Chapter Ten

PRINCIPLE 9:
SOURCING

"If it's to be, it's up to me."

– William H. Johnsen

SOURCING IS THE ninth principle of abundance and prosperity. Sourcing is the consciousness that everything is up to you. If something is going to happen, it's up to you. You see, you're always the source for everything. The question is, what are you sourcing? If you're sourcing joy, love, happiness, health, success, abundance, it's you. If you're sourcing conflict, breakdown, stress, scarcity, once again, it's you.

Sourcing is creating the desired result from a deep level of intention. One who sources embodies all of the principles of abundance and prosperity. If it's to be, it's up to me! I am the cause of *everything*.

Now, this does not mean that everything that goes wrong is your fault. It means that you are the source. You are holding yourself as powerful, capable, and enough. You matter. You can. You are important. You are a unique gift and contribution to this universe.

If I hold myself back, I rip the world off of what I can offer.
If there is going to be love in my life, it is up to me.
If I want more enthusiasm in my world, it's up to me.
If I want joy in my relationships, it's up to me.
If I want freedom, it's up to me.
If I want peace in the world and in my life, it's up to me.

When I stand as source, I create sourcing. That means attracting. I can attract the job, the role, the amazing partner or spouse. I will source the beautiful people, amazing business, money, and support I want.

We get to access abundance and source prosperity into our lives. Sourcing is a place to stand from and a place to operate from.

Sourcing is one of the biggest principles of abundance and prosperity because when we take responsibility for everything, then life shows up differently. It puts us in the driver's seat of our own life. We have the power to create anything we dream of. I am convinced that, as human beings, we can truly have it all. We can have what we want, when we want, where we want, at whatever time we want. It is already meant to be. We were all born to be great. The only way this will happen is by taking 100 percent responsibility for everything in our lives. Once again, what I am speaking about is a platform to operate from: an attitude, a belief, not necessarily a fact.

Often, we confuse responsibility with blame. We think, *It is my fault that my husband cheated on me or that my partner ripped me off. It's totally my fault that my stockbroker put my money in an illegal fund.* Wait a minute! No, that is not my fault, but it's my responsibility. I am responsible for choosing my stockbroker and keeping an eye on my investment portfolio. I am responsible for the partner I chose and should have probably paid more attention to what was going on with the books. I saw the signs that my husband wasn't happy. I failed to show up in the relationship. It was easier to carry on than it was to confront the fact that something was wrong.

Through sourcing, you get the opportunity to look responsibly toward how you might have created the outcome. It's a tool that opens you up for making wiser choices and decisions down the road. What questions did I not ask, or what did I allow to happen? What's the lesson in this for me?

Even if you look back and say, "I couldn't have done anything different," it doesn't matter. There's still a responsible viewpoint for you to embrace. Maybe you're not responsible for it happening, but you're responsible for what you do with what happened. In other words, "I can't change the fact that that happened, but what I do with that—be empowered by it, be inspired by it—that's all on me."

People allow events to define them—for example, divorce, a relationship that didn't work, a job loss, or an injury. Each of these could be the end of something or they could be the beginning of something different. You can either beat yourself up in misery because you lost your job, or you can turn that breakdown into a breakthrough.

Professional athletes do this all of the time. They suffer a career-ending injury and then have to reinvent themselves. Oftentimes, you'll find that they turned an obstacle into an opportunity, a disadvantage into a blessing, and created even greater success by doing something entirely different with their lives. Magic Johnson is an example. A former NBA star diagnosed with HIV in 1991, he could have easily been a victim of his circumstance. He chose to take 100 percent responsibility and turned his pain into purpose. He is now an advocate for HIV/AIDs prevention and has sourced Magic Johnson Enterprises, which is valued at 1 billion dollars, giving Magic Johnson a personal net worth of 500 million dollars.

Had he not taken responsibility for his life, he would easily have become one of thousands of athletes who have a story about why they don't have what they want.

When we see life from the standpoint of responsibility we are sourcing. "I am the source, and I'm responsible for everything." With that perspective and acceptance, we can participate in life in a different way.

You might be thinking, "How am I responsible for something like war in the Middle East?" Naturally, that's not your fault, but what you contribute on a daily basis, whether it's negative or positive, can create war or it can create peace. We are all responsible in some way, big or small, for the big picture.

Sourcing is the idea of attracting to our lives all the things, all the people, and all of the right situations that we say we want, because we're always the source. This brings us to a critical question: What are you sourcing? If you want to source success, if you want to source positive things, then you have to start shifting your viewpoint.

This is a very important principle because being responsible isn't just, "If something is going to happen, it's up to me." It's also, "I'm responsible for how I see the world." Do you see the world as all bad? Or do you see the world as good and generous?

It's an interpretation, and it will affect you, just as the way you interpret things that others say and that, too, affects you. You may not have control over how people treat you, but you always have control over how you respond.

I can't control the economy. I can't control if my boss is having a bad day. I can't control if a client that I've been working with for three months decides to blow me off and go work with someone else. I can't control partners. I can't control anybody outside of me, but true abundance is about self-control. It's about being clear that I am the one who creates the filters of my life, and I can see life through those filters.

I can see life as a victim, blaming everybody (which gets us nowhere, by the way), or I can see life as a blessing and see life as the source. Then, when I come from source, I actually attract the things that I want.

Sourcing activates the law of attraction. Sourcing reminds us that every situation in the past, present, and future is created and attracted by us. The question I am always asking myself is, what am I sourcing? Am I sourcing the health, energy, love, relationships, money, and opportunities I want, or I am sourcing stress, fear, anxiety, drama, scarcity, etc.? If I am not sourcing what I want, then I get to shift how I am showing up in the world. According to Einstein, insanity is repeating the same thing over and over expecting a different result. If you are not sourcing into your life abundance and prosperity, you get to find the missing piece within yourself to source it. Remember always, you have the power to create and attract the life you dream of. At the end of the day, we will either have our results or our stories. Victims have a good story about why they don't have the results they wanted. Abundant and prosperous beings have extraordinary results.

Practice Sourcing

1. Describe who you are committed to being in your life from this point forward so that you can start sourcing and attracting the extraordinary results you want.

In the next section, use the words that you want to be. Pick ten words. For example, I am beautiful, powerful, intelligent, patient, loving, committed, passionate, disciplined, confident, and sexy.

I am:

2. Identify the top ten barriers that you get to challenge and breakthrough to become this person. For example, lack of confidence, fear, distrusting, lack of patience, controlling, lack of discipline, unworthy, lack of integrity, pessimistic, analytical, and shy.

3. Create a plan of action to breakthrough those barriers and develop the qualities.

Example A: Hire a personal coach.
Example B: Listen to Podcasts that empower you in your vision.
Example C: Participate in Emotional Intelligence seminars.
Example D: Apply the 10 principles of Abundance and Prosperity.
Example E: Read books that inspire you, for example:

- *The School of Greatness* by Lewis Howes
- *Living on The Skinny Branches* by Michael Strasner
- *The Art of Acknowledgement* by Margo Majdi
- *Rica…Libertad Financiera Para La Mujer* by Barbara Serrano
- *El Empujoncito Para El Amor* by Maria Marin

TWEET THIS:
"I am the sole and uncontested author of my life."
#TransformYourLife @ChrisMotivador

Chapter Eleven

PRINCIPLE 10:
SURROUND MYSELF WITH
A TEAM

"Surround yourself with people who will lift you higher."
— Oprah

THE FINAL PRINCIPLE, which to me is critical, is to surround myself with a team. Ego thinks, "I don't need anybody," but that's not true. We all need somebody. We're human beings. We need companionship. We need coaches. We need partners. We all need buddies. We all need resources. We all need teachers, guides, and leaders.

I don't mean *need*, like we can't do it alone, because in many instances we can, but there is power in numbers. Alone, I can probably get there, but it will take longer and the result won't be as extraordinary. With a team, I am unstoppable. I will get there quicker, and the result will be extraordinary. If I were to look back at all the accomplishments I am most proud of, they have one thing in common: TEAM. I have been blessed to have always sourced extraordinary people in my life who have stood for me and my vision.

In the first principle, we talked about giving—giving our gifts and talents to others. Why did we do that? What goes around comes around, yes, but there's also another reason. Our value in this world is never validated and recognized until we give it away. Until we share it with others and use it to make a difference in the world, we will never know our true capacity and self-worth.

Now we've come full circle. We've completed the first nine principles and come back to that one thing that we all need—people. We need support, encouragement, advice, guidance, direction, and a cheerleading squad that will root us on until we're celebrating and doing our victory dance. We need someone to correct us when we stray and go in the wrong direction, to give us a hand when we fall. We need the power of many when we are just one.

We need a team. And the best way to find that team is to network. Networking is one of the most powerful tools that we can use in business and in relationships. According to billionaire Warren Buffet, your network is your most valuable asset.

Who is on Your Team?

Let's say you want to be an entrepreneur and it's been a lifelong dream of yours to create a business. Rather than jumping in before you know how to stay afloat, find someone who's already created what you want and learn from them. Ask them to be your mentor. If you want to have a successful relationship, find people who actually created successful relationships. Spend time with them. Watch, listen, observe.

Whatever it is that you're looking for, surround yourself with people who are going to line up with your vision.

If you want to make money, seek accountants, investors, bankers, and financial advisors for their experience and advice.

If you want to be an actor, get an agent and an acting coach. Network with people in the industry. Attend plays, join an acting group, and use your persistence until an experienced actor takes you under their wing and shows you the ropes and the need-to-knows.

Make friends, not enemies. The world is your oyster. There are a whole lot of pearls out there—pearls of wisdom, pillars of society, respected members of the community, business people, spiritual and religious leaders, coaches, advisory councils, mastermind groups, and social networks galore just ready to outflow their gifts and talents to you.

When you join your unique talents with the wisdom, experience, guidance, and support of others, that, my friend, is abundance. That is prosperity.

It's probably not difficult to know instinctively who should be on your team, but what do you do when there are already people in your life who drag you down— the naysayers, doubters, and critics who seem to live for the opportunity to take your dream and stomp on it? It's important to remove toxic people from your life. I'm going to say it again. It's important to remove toxic people from your life. They are barriers that stand in the way of your success. Simply put, you cannot make positive changes in your life when you surround yourself with negativity.

How do you do that without feeling bad? They might be a friend you've had since sixth grade, or maybe they're a family member. What if they're someone you've done a lot of business with throughout the years? How can you possibly remove them from your life without looking and feeling like a heel? Without abandoning them entirely? Or making them feel like you've abandoned them?

Nobody wants to hurt someone else. That goes against our nature. But you can prevent toxic personalities and relationships from influencing you and your future. You do that by being clear that you're not the one removing them, your vision is. That's what I said. Blame your vision. It's got a strong back; it can take it.

My vision is a life of joy and peace and success, and I want to surround myself with joyful, peaceful, successful people. However, I have somebody who's a roadblock in that and who's actually taking from my joy, peace, and success. I need to have "the talk."

What's the talk? The talk is, "I love you. You're a great person and you've been important in my life, but I want you to know that in my life there's no room for anything negative. When you're ready to be positive and you're ready to have a different attitude, welcome back. But until then, I don't want you in my life."

I know it sounds cold, but they don't have a problem being negative in your life. They don't have a problem taking from you. Remember, this is your life, and you're a giving and grateful person! You cannot surround yourself with people who are ungrateful takers. You're sourcing and taking responsibility for your outcomes and results. If you want abundance and prosperity in your life, you have to take responsibility. If you don't remove the toxic people from your life, it's your fault, not theirs, if you don't get the results you want. I have a saying, "Fail me once, shame on you; fail me twice, shame on you; fail me three times, shame on me because I'm the one who is allowing you to fail me."

I think having "the talk" is actually a blessing for them, as well, because we end up enabling people who are like that. By allowing toxic people in your life, you enable them to continue being toxic. You enable them to continue to live in their negativity and misery. Then nothing changes. It's when people realize that they can't get away with things anymore that sometimes breakthroughs happen. Believe it or not, I've seen how this can change people by opening their eyes to how others see them. Suddenly, they see themselves in a different light and start to show up in a different, more positive way.

I hate to say the words "get rid of," because people are not disposable. But I have shifted away from a lot of people in my life who were toxic. Some of them had the biggest breakthroughs because I was no longer available for them. Because of that, they started taking inventory in their lives and they shifted. They had a huge breakthrough, and now they're back in my life, bigger and better than ever before. So remember, part of creating a powerful team of people in your life is to make sure there is space for them. Toxic people take up a lot of space.

The Value of a Team:

It's really important to surround yourself with a team of people who speak the same language, have the same vision, and line up with what you say matters to you, because then you become truly unstoppable in creating the results you want in your life. If someone in your life is taking energy away from you, then, by God, you owe it to you and to your family and the people you love to do something about it.

It's a question of energy. We need all energy. But what kind of energy are you getting? Is it negative energy that drains, depletes, and exhausts you? Or is positive energy that inspires and propels you to move forward? You want all your energy toward your vision, toward your business, toward success, not toward deflecting toxic people who don't support you and your dreams. I recommend surrounding myself with people who will support me in my vision. One of the things that has supported me personally is having a coach. A coach is someone who is on your team and mentors you toward your goals. I have had many coaches in my life. I am eternally grateful to all of them. A coach is someone who does not sell out on you, and they are a relentless maniac on a mission for your success. Coaches always challenge you to step out of your comfort zone and expand yourself so you can source your desired results. I recommend hiring a life coach. There are coaching environments that can support you in developing your emotional intelligence, ways of being, and the beliefs and attitudes that will create personal transformation. Seminars, workshops, and books are all valuable tools to incorporate into your team. A coach is a star maker!

PRACTICE MY TEAM

Having a team with insight, experience, skills, and talents will help you expand your abundance and prosperity. They support you and your goals, while bringing you positive energy to move you toward your vision and dreams.

Make a list below of your top ten most valuable teammates and state what you appreciate about them.

For example:

Name: Ednita Nazario

I appreciate: her never-ending unconditional love and support. She does not sell out on me and celebrates my wins.

(If you cannot come up with 10, this lets you know the work you need to do in this area.)

1. _____

2. _____

3. _____

4. _____

5. _____

6. _____

7. _____

8. _____

9. _____

10. _____

TWEET THIS:
"Individuals play the game, but teams beat
the odds." – Navy Seals
#TransformYourLife @ChrisMotivador

CONCLUSION

I AM OFTEN ASKED, "Wow, so far we've talked about ten principles. It's a lot. How do I apply all of them?"

First, I want you to understand that applying all ten of the principles of abundance and prosperity will change your life. They cannot *not* change your life. These ten principles are game changers. However, I also want you to understand that I know it can be overwhelming to apply all of these principles at once from day one. The good thing is you don't need to apply all of them, just apply one. If you only apply one of these principles, your life will start to see a shift. It's important to know that.

In this book, we've talked about ten powerful, life-changing principles. We've learned how they impact our lives and how they will help us move toward our visions. We've learned how to use the universe as our friend, not our enemy, and place trust in ourselves and the world around us.

We've learned to operate from a place of responsibility and integrity, where character counts and makes a difference. We've learned how to give, fully and freely, of the many unique gifts and talents that are housed in every one of us. We've learned how to break the cycle of scarcity as we travel toward greater riches and rewards.

Above all, we've learned that nothing is impossible. Remember, if it's to be, it's up to me. Nobody can make you feel bad without your permission. We've heard that many times. It's also true that you cannot succeed without your own permission, and nobody can get in your way unless you let them.

Your future is now. Starting right now at this very minute you are one second more in the future than you were when you read the last sentence. Every tick of the clock will bring it closer to you. When the future arrives, what will it look like? Where will you be? Who will you be with? What will you be doing? And how will it feel?

I can tell you right now that it will feel amazing. It will bring you to your feet and fill your eyes with tears of gratitude. You'll feel worthy and valuable and emboldened with the power of the universe at your back. Your gifts and talents will expand and multiply, making you richer in spirit than you can imagine.

I know you can do it. I did, and I wasn't a believer. It's amazing how it happened, almost as if things started falling into place right before my eyes. Sure, it took commitment and dedication, but, along the way, it became easier. This is the life I wish for you—a life that graces you with the things that matter most to you.

Your ten-year action plan starts right now, at this very minute.

Make it happen. Make it amazing. Make it yours.

Transform Your Life: 10 Principles of Abundance and Prosperity is a 1-Day workshop facilitated by Chris Lee and offered worldwide.

To register for the workshop, go to
www.ChrisLeeMotivator.com

To host a workshop or to hire Chris Lee as your personal and business coach, go to ChrisLeeMotivator.com/contactus

ACKNOWLEDGEMENTS

THIS BOOK EXISTS because of my family and extended family of friends and colleagues. I thank my mother and my stepfather, Dave, because without them, I would not be where I am today. Thank you to my brothers and sister, Michael, Andy, Jeffrey and Robin. You have all contributed to my life in a special way. To Michael Strasner, for being my friend and partner in transformation. Thank you to all the center owners for your faith and trust in me and creating a space to transform people's lives: To Mario Huertas, thank you for believing in me and this project from the beginning – you are the best. Claudette, my unconditional friend that is always there for me. To Luz Garcia, Hermana te adoro. To Robyn (twin), Corrine (evil twin), Margo (sister), Roger, Chris Hawker, Sommer Renaldo, Abraham Alexander, Perla, Lupita – thank you. To Impacto Vital, you are my heart. Additional thanks to Ivette Rodriguez (dentist) and Ivette Rodriguez (trainer) To all my graduates in the Dominican Republic; Bogota, Columbia; Quito, Ecuador; and Seville and Madrid, Spain, thank you. Thank you to all my mentors, including Micky McQuaid and James P. Cook. Special thanks to Lewis Howes, your transformation inspires me every day. To Alicia Dunams, without you, this book would not exist—you are the book whisperer. Toccara, thank you for your love and support. To my tribe of friends, you inspire me every single day. My life would be nothing without you. Ednita Nazario, you are my soul mate, Carolina Marquez, my oxygen. Reymond Collazo gracias por tu amor y la foto de la portada. Celeste Esparza my lifelong Bff. Alexandra Malagon, thank you for being my partner in this journey with Gilberto Santa Rosa. To my love, Barbara Bermudo, you inspire me. Mario Andres Moreno, the best dad in the world. Maria Marin, you are an inspiration. To Alejandro Martinez, my life buddy. Dauset Vazquez, my partner in crime. To Daniel & Alejandra, thank you for being my family. Pauley Shore, your heart is even bigger than your smile. Love to my sisters, Maritza Casiano, and Grace Marie Herger and my adopted daughter, Agatha Gomez. To my God Daughter, Ana Sophia Garcia – I'm proud of you. Thanks also to my BFFs: Vivi Santiestaban, Barbara Serrano, Nadine Velasquez, and my brother Julian Gill. Extra thanks to Daniel Negraneu and Silverio Perez. Much thanks to all my dear friends and loved ones who have contributed to my life and this book.

ABOUT THE AUTHOR - CHRIS LEE

PASSIONATE, VISIONARY, OUTRAGEOUS, and committed are few of the words that describe Chris Lee. A man on a mission committed to transforming the world one heart at a time. Chris Lee has spent over 25 years of his life transforming the lives of thousands of people worldwide through his workshops, coaching, and participation in all media, teaching people how to live an abundant prosperous life. Born in Huntington, NY and grew up in San Juan, PR where he faced many challenges growing up that have led to life lessons he has been able to share with others. While attending Northeastern University, where he studied Speech Communications and Psychology, he found his life calling when he participated in an emotional intelligence seminar. After graduating college, he pursued a career as a transformational trainer and facilitator. This opportunity brought him around the world. Chris Lee has led seminars in Russia, Hong Kong, China, Taiwan, Australia, USA, and Latin America. He is the author of the best seller " Dile Yes! A la VIDA." Chris is also creator of "The Torch Workshop", a leadership seminar for teenagers 13-17 years old that has been offered to thousands of adolescents around the world. He has led corporate workshops for hundreds of corporations such as "Coca Cola", "Unilever", "Amgen", "Proctor and Gamble", "National Insurance", "Miss Universe" and many others. Chris Lee has hosted radio, television shows, and podcasts worldwide such as: Univision's "Despierta America", "Nuestra Belleza Latina" and "El Show de Zuleyka"; Venevision's "Arquitecto de Suenos", Telemundo's "Dia a Dia" and "Noticiero de Telemundo." Chris Lee can currently be heard nationwide on Univision's "Maria Marin Live" and can also be heard on Lewis Howes' podcast " The School of Greatness." Find out more about Chris Lee at www.ChrisLeeMotivator.com

51287316R00087

Made in the USA
Middletown, DE
10 November 2017